¡Es Español!

Kathy Williams
and
Beatriz Rubio

Brilliant Publications

Publisher's information

Published by Brilliant Publications,
Unit 10,
Sparrow Hall Farm,
Edlesborough, Dunstable,
Bedfordshire LU6 2ES.

Sales and stock enquiries:
Tel: 01202 712910
Fax: 0845 1309300
e-mail: brilliant@bebc.co.uk
website: www.brilliantpublications.co.uk

General information enquiries:
Tel: 01525 222292

The name 'Brilliant Publications' and the logo are registered trademarks.

Written by Kathy Williams and Beatriz Rubio
Illustrated by Chantel Kees
Printed by Dardedze Holography in Latvia
© Kathy Williams and Beatriz Rubio
ISBN 978 1 903853 64 1 (This book is sold together with a CD; the book and CD are not available separately.)
First published 2004, reprinted 2007.
10 9 8 7 6 5 4 3 2

Introduction

Es Español is designed for non-specialist teachers of foreign languages. The scheme aims to encourage primary school pupils to enjoy learning Spanish, and to communicate in speech and writing through the acquisition of simple grammar and a variety of vocabulary.

Each of the 18 units has teachers' notes and photocopiable pupil worksheets. Each unit addresses several learning objectives, allowing for the material to be taught over several lessons or as a whole. Grammar teaching is approached through the context of the unit theme, for example 'un/una' in the context of animals and adjectives in the unit about clothes. There is progression through the units, but they can equally be selected for use in a different order, to complement classwork in maths or English, for example.

The 'Key words – Vocabulario' in the teachers' notes for each unit contain the language that pupils should learn. Frequent references are made to relevant units elsewhere in the book where the same key language also appears. Additional vocabulary may be required to meet pupils' particular interests and some of the activities require the use of a Spanish–English dictionary.

The 'Activities' sections are written as suggested lessons and provide readily accessible teaching plans that can be adapted and altered to suit individual needs. The 'Further activities' are not always more difficult; they provide further suggested ways of working within the unit if more time is available, and include ideas for successful classroom displays, as well as larger group or whole school exercises. All the worksheets may be adapted and modified to suit individual pupils. Several are designed to be cut up to make flashcards or games. These sheets would benefit from enlargement and/or lamination.

The 'Appendix' includes notes on basic grammar points raised in the units and some relevant background information. A complete listing of the 'Key words – Vocabulario' is on pages 118–120.

A CD accompanies this book to help non-specialist teachers to teach Spanish by modelling pronunciation, providing questions for comprehension and giving model answers. Where the CD is part of the lesson plan the symbol 𝄞 is shown on the teachers' notes. In addition the CD contains seven traditional Spanish songs. English translations of the songs can be found on page 117.

Many opportunities exist to link the study of Spanish through Es Español to other curriculum areas: literacy and numeracy, ICT, technology, geography, music, art and sport. Pupils can collaborate with others in pairs and groups and expand their cultural awareness. Above all, pupils can experience through learning a foreign language a sense of personal achievement which they can carry forward into their secondary school language learning.

Contents

Unit 1

Hola

Learning objectives

Pupils will be able to:

* ✱ Say hello and introduce themselves
* ✱ Greet people
* ✱ Use the alphabet in Spanish

Resources needed

* ✱ Sheets 1a, 1b, 1c; CD Track 1
* ✱ Spanish name cards.

Vocabulario – Key words

hola	hello
adiós	goodbye
me llamo …	my name is …
¿cómo estás?	how are you?
bien	I'm fine
gracias	thank you
¿cómo te llamas?	
	what is your name?

Activities

* ✱ Introduce 'Hola'. Pupils repeat the word. You could move around the class and shake hands with individuals saying 'Hola', encouraging them to reply. Explain greeting customs: shaking hands, kissing on both cheeks.

* ✱ Introduce '¿Cómo te llamas?' for recognition, and reply 'Me llamo …' Pause the CD to allow the children to respond. On Sheet 1a pupils can fill in their picture frame and copy the sentences.

* ✱ Introduce the phrases '¿Cómo estás?' and 'Bien, gracias.' Pupils repeat the question and answer. They could question each other and give the response.

* ✱ Introduce 'Adiós', Pupils repeat it. Mix with 'Hola' to practise.

* ✱ Distribute cards from sheet 1b. Pupils say the word or phrase that they have on their card. Work together to build up a dialogue together by putting the phrases into a logical sequence. Sheet 1c gives a completed dialogue.

* ✱ Listen to the alphabet in Spanish. Spell the name of someone in the class in Spanish – first person to guess the name correctly wins a point. Play in teams. Pupils could take the role of caller. Listen to how 'España' and 'español' are pronounced on the tape. Repeat with the children until they learn this particular Spanish sound which does not have an equivalent in English.

* ✱ Pupils spell out their own names for a partner to write exactly as they say. They could use Spanish name cards for additional practice.

Further activities

* ✱ Give each pupil a card with a 'new' Spanish name. They introduce themselves using 'Me llamo …' (see sheet 6a for sample names).

* ✱ Pupils 'meet' each other around the group using as many phrases as possible in a conversation (with or without reference to sheet 1c). The question '¿Cómo te llamas?' could be incorporated into the dialogues.

* ✱ Using photographs, pupils mount their picture with 'Hola, me llamo …' beneath it, round it, etc. Make a class display.

www.brilliantpublications.co.uk   ¡Es Español!   © Kathy Williams and Beatriz Rubio

Hola

Hello

Hola.
Me llamo Sofía.

Hola.
Me llamo Javier.

Dibújate y copia las frases:

Draw yourself and copy the sentences:

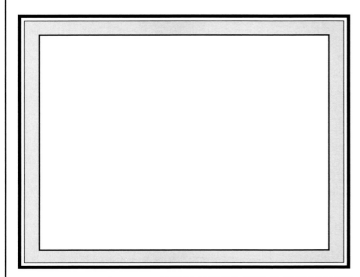

_____

_____   _____

_____

Di

Say

✂

di: **Hello** say:	di: **How are you?** say:
di: **I'm very well** say:	di: **Thank you** say:
di: **My name is …** say:	di: **Goodbye** say:

¡Es Español!   © *Kathy Williams and Beatriz Rubio*

Una conversación

A conversation

Learning objectives

Pupils will be able to:

✹ Understand and use some classroom instructions and language

✹ Name some common school equipment

Resources needed

✹ Sheets 2a, 2b; CD Track 2

✹ School equipment, eg pencil, pen, ruler; cloth/tea towel; tray.

Activities

✹ 👂 Pupils respond to the instructions on the CD by doing the actions required. Through mime and gestures they can interpret the instructions 'stand up','sit down', 'look', 'listen' and 'repeat'. They hear 'Muy bien' after each successful response.

✹ 👂 Introduce the phrase 'Perdone'. There are opportunities to practise its use later in the Unit.

✹ You could give a series of instructions for a game of 'Juan dice'. Just as in 'Simon says' the pupils should respond only if you say 'Juan dice' in front of the instructions.

✹ Pupils could choose one or more of the instructions to design as a poster for classroom reference.

✹ 👂 Pupils will see examples of instructions that they will come across in the course on sheet 2a. The instructions can also be heard on the CD. Explain how instructions to a group end in '-ad', '-ed' or '-id'.

Vocabulario – Key words

sentaos	sit down
levantaos	stand up
escuchad	listen
mirad	watch/look
repetid	repeat
completa	complete
haz	do
une	match
copia	copy
lee	read
dibuja	draw
responde	answer
rellena	fill in
escribe	write
encuentra	find
muy bien	very good
perdone	excuse me
sí	yes
no	no
es	it is/this is
un lápiz	a pencil
un bolígrafo	a pen
una cartera	a school bag
un cuaderno	an exercise book
un sacapuntas	a sharpener
una regla	a ruler
un estuche	a pencil case
una goma	a rubber

¿cómo se dice en español? what is this in Spanish?

¡Es Español!   © *Kathy Williams and Beatriz Rubio*

✻ ᕲ Use the CD to introduce objects used in the classroom (see Vocabulario). Place a variety of school equipment (pen, pencil, etc) on a tray or desk. Pick items up to say 'Es un bolígafo' – pupils repeat if the object is 'un bolígrafo' or correct you if it is not. Use 'Sí, es un bolígrafo' or 'No, es un ...'. You could explain here the use of the indefinite article un/una. It is dealt with more fully in Unit 5 (see also Appendix).

✻ Cover the equipment on the tray with a cloth and remove one item from underneath. The pupils must guess which is missing once the cloth is removed.

✻ A matching game is on sheet 2b; pupils have to write the names of items used at school.

✻ ᕲ Explain to the pupils that 'Perdone' can be used if you do not have something. Listen to the CD. 'Perdone' is repeated with 'No tengo bolígrafo/lápiz', etc. Encourage the pupils to question each other.

✻ Play a version of 'The Generation Game' final memory game. Pupils watch as a series of school items is shown (moving conveyor belt not compulsory!). One pupil then volunteers to say them in the order that they appeared. To make it harder, items may appear more than once in the sequence. Start off with a few items, introducing further items as the pupils get more confident.

Further activities

✻ ᕲ Pupils could label further items around the room, eg la puerta = door, la ventana = window, la pizarra = the black/whiteboard. Encourage the use of the phrase '¿Cómo se dice en español?' (modelled on the CD) to find Spanish translations for English words.

✻ Pupils could use 'Es mío' = 'That's mine', Collect pencils and books from the pupils , hold each item up separately for the children to name. The pupil who owns the item says: 'Es mío', Note that if the item is feminine, such as 'una goma' (a rubber) or 'una regla' (a ruler), the pupils will have to say 'Es mía'.

En clase

In the classroom

| Rellena | los espacios. | _____ the gaps. |

| Escribe | los nombres. | _____ the names. |

 Phil

| Une |

Une los animales con sus nombres en español:

un pez

un gato

| Escucha | ---------------- | Responde | _____ |

Escucha el CD.

Responde a las preguntas.
¿Tienes un amigo? Sí.

| Lee | _____ | Completa | _____ |

Lee el texto.

Completa la lista.
1, 2, __ , 4, 5__.

| Dibuja | _____ | Encuentra | _____ |

Dibuja una casa.

Encuentra la palabra 'hola'.

A	S	B	D	M	O	E
A	X	O	E	C	B	D
L	A	H	O	L	A	F
G	B	E	K	D	F	G
H	C	V	E	R	J	H

¡Es Español! © Kathy Williams and Beatriz Rubio

Mis cosas de clase

My things at school

Une los objetos con los alumnos:

Match the objects and pupils:

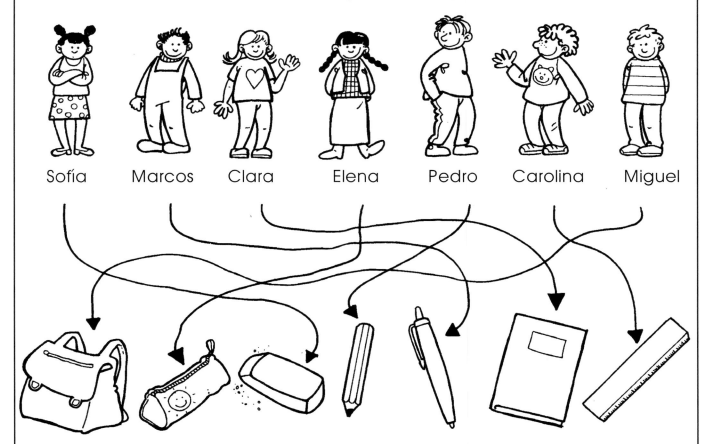

Sofía   Marcos   Clara   Elena   Pedro   Carolina   Miguel

Completa las frases:

Complete the sentences:

Sofía tiene _____ . Sofía

Marcos tiene _____ .

Clara tiene _____ .

Elena tiene _____ .

Pedro tiene _____ .

Carolina tiene_____ .

Miguel tiene _____ .

un bolígrafo	una regla	una goma	un lápiz
un estuche	un cuaderno	una cartera	

La semana

Learning objectives

Pupils will be able to:

* Recognize and use days of the week

Resources needed

* Sheets 3a, 3b
* Calendar; card; A4 transparent file pockets; sticky notelets or paper and Blu-Tack; cork tiles; drawing pins.

Vocabulario – Key words

lunes	Monday
martes	Tuesday
miércoles	Wednesday
jueves	Thursday
viernes	Friday
sábado	Saturday
domingo	Sunday
los días (de)	the days (of)
la semana	the week
hoy	today

Activities

* Introduce the days of the week (pointing at days on a calendar as pupils hear them in Spanish). In Spanish it is customary to list the days of the week starting with 'lunes' (Monday).

* Pupils say what day it is 'today' ('hoy'). Continue with suggested activities for particular days to elicit Spanish name: eg perhaps pupils have music on Tuesday or swimming on Friday. You could mime the activities: there may be several correct answers!

* Pupils fill in sheet 3a with a typical activity for each day.

Further activities

* Pupils mime activities to partner to guess day.

* Pupils could make a weekly reminder board to take home (photocopy sheet 3b onto A4 sized paper or card). The day boxes could be illustrated/ decorated. Put the A4 paper/card into a transparent pocket. Sticky notelets or paper with Blu-Tack can be used to put messages/reminders onto relevant days. At the end of the week the plan is reusable! An alternative design would be to use a cork tile. Stick or write the days of the week on the tile and pin messages as required.

¡Es Español! © Kathy Williams and Beatriz Rubio

Los días de la semana

The days of the week

Dibuja una cosa que haces en cada uno de los días.

Draw something that you do on each day.

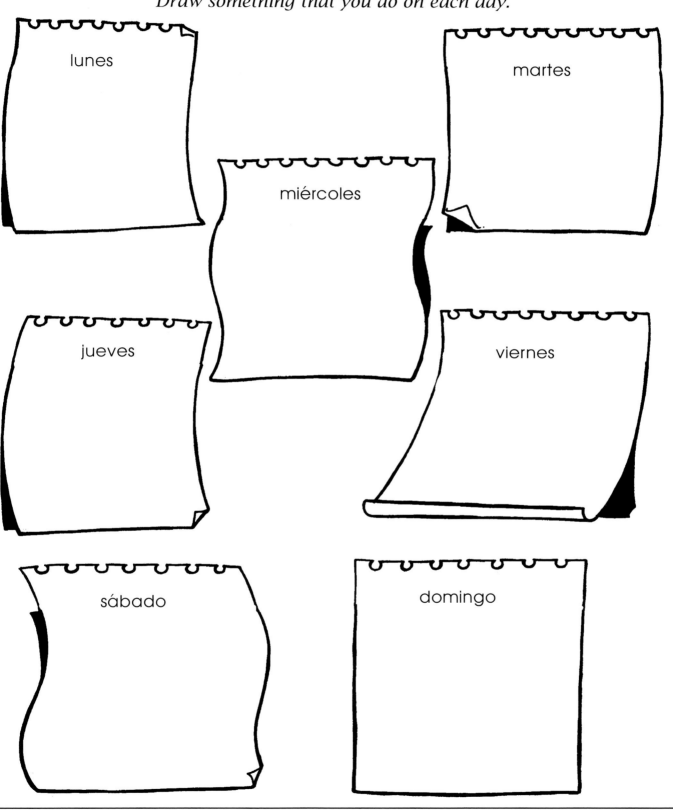

   www.brilliantpublications.co.uk

Los días de la semana

The days of the week

lunes	martes

miércoles	jueves

viernes	sábado

domingo	

lunes

martes

miércoles

jueves

viernes

sábado

domingo

¡Es Español! © Kathy Williams and Beatriz Rubio

Las estaciones y el tiempo

Learning objectives

Pupils will be able to:

* Talk about the weather and seasons in general
* Describe the day's weather conditions

Resources needed

* Sheets 4a, 4b, 4c, 4d, 4e; CD Tracks 4–5
* Cardboard; split pins; large sheet of paper; sticky notelets or paper and Blu-Tack.

Activities

*) Introduce weather expressions. Listen to the CD and show the flashcards (sheet 4a) as they are heard. Pupils repeat the phrases.

Vocabulario – Key words	
en primavera	in spring
en verano	in summer
en otoño	in autumn
en invierno	in winter
llueve	it rains/is raining
nieva	it snows/is snowing
hace bueno	it is fine
hace sol	it is sunny
hace malo	it is not a nice day
hace calor	it is hot
hace frío	it is cold
hace viento	it is windy
¿qué tiempo hace?	what is the weather like?
hoy	today

* Use the flashcards to emphasize weather expressions. Place flashcards in a row face down on a table/board. One pupil picks a card, gives it to you without looking at it and has a guess at the weather expression. If incorrect then the group can guess. The correct pupil chooses another card, and so on.

* Pupils fill in the weather wheel (sheet 4b) by putting the correct phrase(s) with the pictures. They could mount it on cardboard and put a split pin through the middle with the arrow cut out. Highlight repetition of 'Hace ...'

*) Introduce the question '¿Qué tiempo hace hoy?' Pupils move the arrow to point to today's weather and respond. They could also point and say the weather for other days as if they were back on that day.

*) Introduce seasons by extending '¿Qué tiempo hace ... en otoño/en invierno?' Suggest several typical weather conditions and actions to help elicit understanding of season words. Repeat, eg 'En otoño hace viento y llueve.' Pupils suggest weather typical of each season.

* Sheet 4c can be used to reinforce the seasons.

*) Sheet 4d. This listening exercise combines seasons and weather. Pupils number the pictures as they hear the corresponding descriptions. More able pupils could write the phrases as well.

✱ 🎧   Sheet 4e (CD Track 5). Song: ¡Qué llueva, qué llueva! Pupils could follow the words and sing the song.

Further activities

✱   Pupils could use a chart similar to 'la semana' week plan (Unit 3) to record the weather each day for a week either by writing the phrase or drawing a weather symbol. On Friday you could review the week's weather.

✱   Weather 'round-up'. Draw a large outline of Spain on the board/large sheet of paper. Mark on a few principal towns, eg Madrid, Barcelona, Málaga, Valencia, etc (sheet 6b could be enlarged). Pupils prepare weather symbols in pairs/groups on sticky notelets or small pieces of paper and Blu-Tack. They then present a weather 'round-up' saying 'En Madrid llueve', or 'En Barcelona, hace bueno', etc while sticking their symbols on the map.

El tiempo (flashcards)

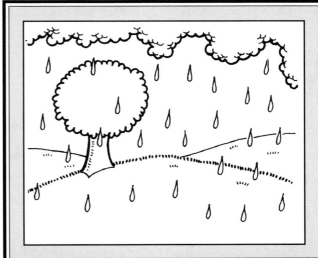

¿Qué tiempo hace hoy?

What is the weather like today?

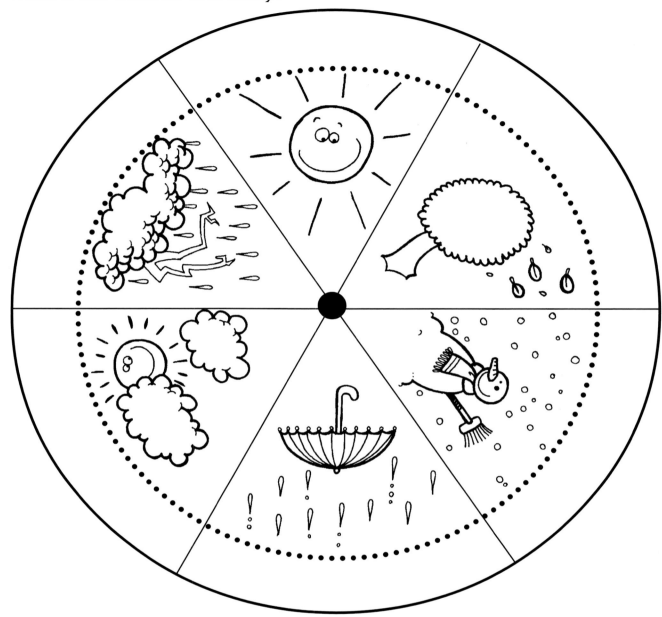

Une las frases y los dibujos.

Match the phrases and pictures.

hace sol	llueve
hace viento	hace frío
hace malo	hace calor
hace bueno	nieva

Corta la flecha y colócala en el centro.

Cut out the arrow and put it in the middle.

¡Es Español!   © Kathy Williams and Beatriz Rubio

Las estaciones

The seasons

Dibuja algo de cada estación.
Draw something for each season.

verano

primavera

otoño

invierno

www.brilliantpublications.co.uk

¿Qué tiempo hace en verano?

What is the weather like in summer?

👂 **Escucha y escribe el número que corresponda.**

Listen and write the number.

¡Es Español!   © Kathy Williams and Beatriz Rubio

¡Qué llueva, qué llueva!

Let's hope it rains, it rains!

Canta esta canción.

Sing this song.

¡Qué llueva, qué llueva!

La Virgen de la cueva

Los pajaritos cantan

Las nubes se levantan

¡Qué sí, qué no, qué caiga un chaparrón!

¡Qué caiga un chaparrón, con azúcar y limón!

www.brilliantpublications.co.uk

Unit 5

Los números 0-20

Learning objectives

Pupils will be able to:

✱ Count to 20
✱ Recognize the use of un/una as indefinite article (masculine or feminine)

Resources needed

✱ Sheets 5a, 5b, 5c, 5d; CD Tracks 6–7
✱ Pencils, sweets, toys, bricks, etc for counting; hat.

Activities

Part A

✱ 👂 Listen to and practise numbers from 0–10. Pupils could use fingers to count and repeat.

✱ 👂 Using ten pencils, sweets, or toys, ask pupils in turn to hand you something, eg 'Dame tres gomas.' When a pupil has chosen the correct number of pencils, return them to the set and start again. Divide pupils into groups and let them ask the questions. Note: On the CD you will hear 'dame' which is the correct form for the informal you, in Spanish 'tú'. The polite form corresponding to 'usted' would be 'deme'. When a teaher is addressing a single child 'dame' is the correct form.

✱ Use sheets 5a and 5b together. Cut 5a into ten separate cards. Pupils can then stick the written numbers over the grid. Highlight how 'c' in 'cuatro' is a 'k' sound, but the first 'c' in 'cinco' sounds like 'th' in 'think'.

Part B

✱ 👂 Listen to and practise numbers from 11–15. Encourage the pupils to repeat.

✱ Give each pupil a number between 11 and 15. Ask all the pupils to stand up to start the game. As you say a number, the pupils repeat it and sit down if it is their number. The winner(s) are those left standing at the end.

Vocabulario – Key words	
uno	1
dos	2
tres	3
cuatro	4
cinco	5
seis	6
siete	7
ocho	8
nueve	9
diez	10
once	11
doce	12
trece	13
catorce	14
quince	15
dieciséis	16
diecisiete	17
dieciocho	18
diecinueve	19
veinte	20
un/una	one/a/an
por favor	please
dame	give me

¡Es Español!

✴ 🦻 Introduce numbers up to 20. Show pupils ten items (sweets, etc) or use fingers then add 'más' seven, then eight, then nine. Pupils say the numbers ten and seven; you highlight the formation of number 16 as 'diez y seis' (ten and six). Repeat for '17', '18' and '19'. Introduce 20 = viente.

✴ Sheet 5c can be used to reinforce all the numbers. Highlight how a/an can be 'un' or 'una' because words are either masculine or feminine (see Appendix). You could refer pupils back to school equipment (sheet 2b) to check understanding.

✴ 🦻 Song: Un elefante (CD Track 7). This song practises numbers. How many numbers can the pupils remember? Use finger-counting or ask pupils to sing numbers along with the CD. Sheet 5d allows pupils to fill in the numbers while following the song.

Further activities

✴ Using the question '¿Cuántos/cuántas … hay?' ask pupils to count items in the classroom to give a numerical response.

✴ Play 'Loto'. Pupils draw a noughts and crosses grid and choose numbers 0–20 to put on it. Call out numbers from a hat (you or a pupil); the pupils cross them out as they hear them. The winner is the first to have all nine numbers crossed out and to have called 'Loto!'.

✴ Make up mathematical sums and ask pupils to give the solution in Spanish. Here are some examples:

English	Spanish	Sum in words	In numbers
add	más	diez más tres	10 + 3
subtract	menos	once menos siete	11 − 7
multiply by	por	dos por cinco	2 x 5
divide by	entre	doce entre seis	12 ÷ 6
equals	igual a	tres por dos igual a seis	3 x 2 = 6

✴ Use the grid on sheet 5b as number flashcards for a simple game. Give each pupil a number card and call out a number at random. The pupil with that card has to stand up and call another number. This continues until all pupils are standing; the last one to stand up is the winner.

Los números 1–10

Numbers 1-10

cuatro	siete
diez	uno
dos	cinco
seis	ocho
nueve	tres

¡Es Español!   © *Kathy Williams and Beatriz Rubio*

Los números (cuadro)

Numbers (grid)

1	2
3	4
5	6
7	8
9	10

¡Es Español!

www.brilliantpublications.co.uk

Contemos hasta 20

Let's count up to 20

Completa los números. Rellana los espacios.

Complete the numbers. Fill in the gaps.

Remember: some words are feminine and others are masculine. The word for apple is a feminine word, so we add an 'a' on to the end of 'un'.

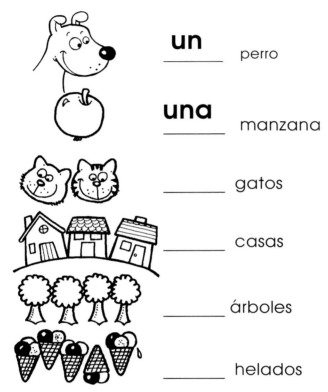

un _____ perro

una _____ manzana

_____ gatos

_____ casas

_____ árboles

_____ helados

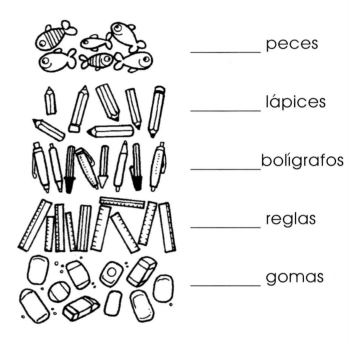

_____ peces

_____ lápices

_____ bolígrafos

_____ reglas

_____ gomas

Une los números con su equivalente en inglés:

Match the numbers to the English:

once	thirteen
doce	eleven
trece	fourteen
catorce	twelve
quince	fifteen

Suma:

Do the addition:

diez + seis = **dieciséis**
10   6

diez + siete = _____
10   7

diez + ocho = _____
10   8

diez + nueve = _____
10   9

diez + diez = _____
10   10

Un elefante

One elephant

Canta esta canción.
Sing this song.

Un elefante se balanceaba sobre la tela de una araña
Como veía que se resistía se fue a llamar a otro elefante.

Dos elefantes se balanceaban sobre la tela de una araña
Como veían que se resistía fueron a llamar a otro elefante.

_____ elefantes se balanceaban sobre la tela de una araña
Como veían que se resistía fueron a llamar a otro elefante.

_____ elefantes se balanceaban sobre la tela de una araña
Como veían que se resistía fueron a llamar a otro elefante.

_____ elefantes se balanceaban sobre la tela de una araña
Como veían que se resistía fueron a llamar a otro elefante.

_____ elefantes se balanceaban sobre la tela de una araña
Como veían que se resistía fueron a llamar a otro elefante.

_____ elefantes se balanceaban sobre la tela de una araña
Como veían que se resistía fueron a llamar a otro elefante.

_____ elefantes se balanceaban sobre la tela de una araña
Como veían que se resistía fueron a llamar a otro elefante.

_____ elefantes se balanceaban sobre la tela de una araña
Como veían que se resistía fueron a llamar a otro elefante.

Me presento

Learning objectives

Pupils will be able to:

✳ Say where they live
✳ Identify some town names and locations in Spain
✳ Say their address
✳ Use numbers in addresses

Resources needed:

✳ Sheet 6a, 6b, 6c; CD Track 8
✳ Map of Spain with cities, rivers, mountains, regions marked; card.

Vocabulario – Key words

me llamo ...	my name is ...
¿dónde vives?	where do you live?
vivo en ...	I live in ...
mi dirección es ...	my address is ...

Activities

✳ ♪ The characters on sheet 6a are introduced on the CD, using 'Me llamo ...' and 'Vivo en ...', together with the names of some Spanish towns/cities and London (Londres). Pupils could cut out the town names and match them to people when they hear them on the CD. Alternatively use a large outline map of Spain and stick people/town names on to the map together. Sheet 6b reinforces 'Vivo en ...' and the names of Spanish towns. Pupils write the correct numbers in the boxes when they hear the phrases.

✳ ♪ Introduce '¿Dónde vives?' Pupils answer using their own town name, eg 'Vivo en Reading'. You could extend practice by giving the character pictures to pupils; they recall where each person lives from map 6b and use 'Vivo en ...' You could revise 'Me llamo ...' at the same time.

✳ ♪ Introduce 'Mi dirección es ...'. Pupils use numbers (see Unit 5) to say their address if it includes a house number (for numbers 20+ refer to Units 8 and 14).

✳ Ask pupils to fill in sheet 6c. See if they can work out the meaning of the question at the bottom of the sheet. 'La casa' is the theme of the next unit. You could talk about how many Spanish people live in flats or 'pisos' in Madrid, and elsewhere in Spain.

Further activities

✳ Look at a map of Spain and identify additional main towns and cities. You could locate other principal geographical landmarks such as Los Pirineos, Sierra Nevada, El Mar Mediterráneo, Andalucía, Cataluña, etc. You could extend this to a study of one of these landmarks/areas. Have any of the pupils visited Spain?

✳ Give pupils cards with a 'new' address, including a 'new' town. Ask them '¿Dónde vives?' and '¿Cuál es tu dirección?' Alternatively prompt pupils to ask each other and answer using 'Vivo en .... Mi dirección es ...'.

¡Es Español! © Kathy Williams and Beatriz Rubio

Gente (flashcards)

Londres
Madrid
Barcelona
Sevilla
Málaga
La Coruña
Santander
Valencia

James

Lucía

Miguel

Clara

Pedro

María

Marcos

Elena

© Kathy Williams and Beatriz Rubio   ¡Es Español!   31

   www.brilliantpublications.co.uk

Me presento

I'd like to introduce myself

Escucha y escribe el número
Listen and write in the number.

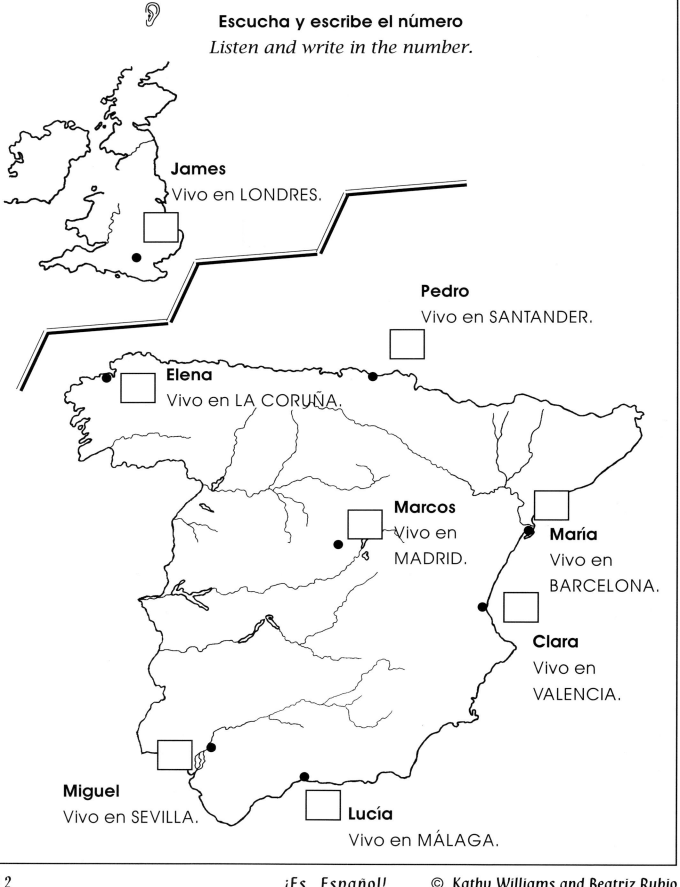

James
Vivo en LONDRES.

Pedro
Vivo en SANTANDER.

Elena
Vivo en LA CORUÑA.

Marcos
Vivo en MADRID.

María
Vivo en BARCELONA.

Clara
Vivo en VALENCIA.

Miguel
Vivo en SEVILLA.

Lucía
Vivo en MÁLAGA.

¡Es Español!   © Kathy Williams and Beatriz Rubio

¿Dónde vives?

Where do you live?

Responde a las preguntas.

Answer the questions.

Vivo en Madrid.

¿Dónde vives?

_____

Mi dirección es Calle Alcalá, 8 Madrid

José Liñan
Calle Alcalá 8
Madrid

¿Cuál es tu dirección?

_____

Vivo en una casa.

¿Vives en una casa o en un apartamento?

_____

En casa

Learning objectives

Pupils will be able to:

★ Say what rooms are in their house, using 'hay'
★ Say which room someone is 'in'
★ Recognize the use of el/la as the definite article 'the' with masculine or feminine words
★ Say what is in their bedroom

Resources needed

★ Sheets 7a, 7b, 7c; CD Track 9
★ Pictures of rooms cut from magazines.

Activities

★ ♪ Using sheet 7a as flashcards, introduce room words.

★ Hide a single card behind a larger card and slowly reveal a part of it. Pupils guess which room is appearing.

★ Mime activities relating to each room. Pupils guess the room. They could do this in pairs or as a group.

Vocabulario – Key words	
la cocina	the kitchen
el dormitorio	the bedroom
el comedor	the dining room
el cuarto de baño	the bathroom
el sótano	the cellar
el salón	the lounge
el ático	the attic
el vestíbulo	the hall
el garaje	the garage
el (masculine word)	the
la (feminine word)	the
en	in
hay	there is/are
una cama	a bed
una alfombra	a rug
un armario	a wardrobe
una mesa	a table
una silla	a chair
¿dónde está …?	where is …?

★ Highlight 'el/la': both mean 'the'. Group the words into those that are feminine (la) and those that are masculine (el) (see Vocabulario). (For more information, see the Appendix.)

★ ♪ Listen to the description of a house using 'En mi casa hay …' Ask pupils to describe their own houses.

★ ♪ Introduce the question '¿Dónde está …?'. Pupils listen and answer questions on sheet 7b orally (then in writing if required) to practise room words.

★ ♪ Sheet 7c introduces some common bedroom furniture words. Pupils could design a bedroom by cutting out the furniture and positioning it on the plan. They could use a dictionary to look up the Spanish words for further items and include them as well.

✳   They could present their finished plans describing their bedrooms using 'En mi dormitorio hay …'.

Further activities

✳   Using cut-out pictures from magazines pupils could mount their pictures on a page, labelling the rooms 'la cocina', 'el dormitorio', etc. They could title the page 'Se vende' (for sale) and make a house particulars sheet from an imaginary 'inmobiliaria' (Estate Agent). A picture of the exterior of a house could complete the advertisement.

✳   Make a display board with 'adverts' framed to look like an agency window.

En casa

In the house (flashcards)

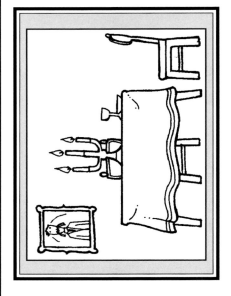

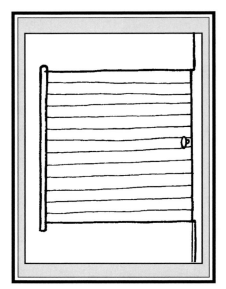

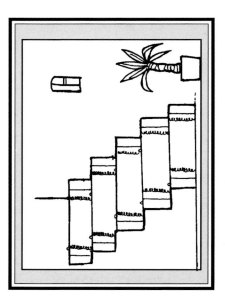

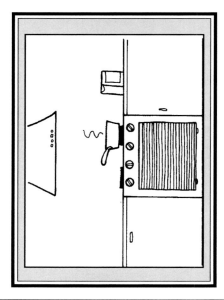

¡Es Español! © Kathy Williams and Beatriz Rubio

¿Dónde está Pedro?

Where is Pedro?

Escucha y rellana los espacios.
Listen and fill in the gaps.

¿Dónde está Pedro? En   **el dormitorio**

¿Dónde está María? En _____

¿Dónde está mamá? En _____

¿Dónde está papá? En _____

¿Dónde está Luis? En _____

¿Dónde está el perro? En _____

¿Dónde está el gato? En _____

¿Dónde está la araña? En _____

¿Dónde está el ratón? En _____

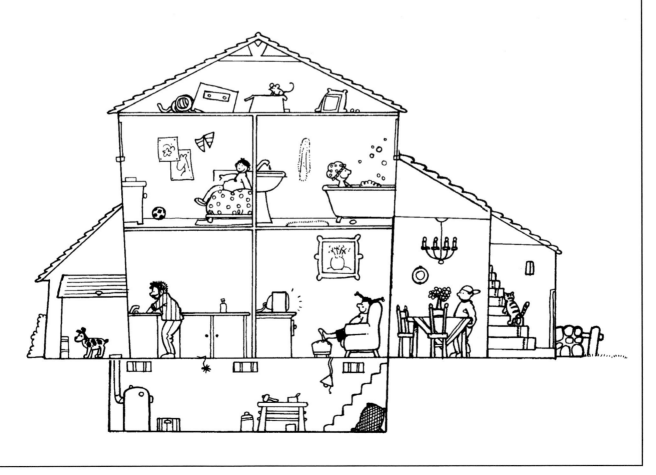

En mi habitación

In my bedroom

Éste es un plano de tu dormitorio.

Here is a plan of your bedroom.

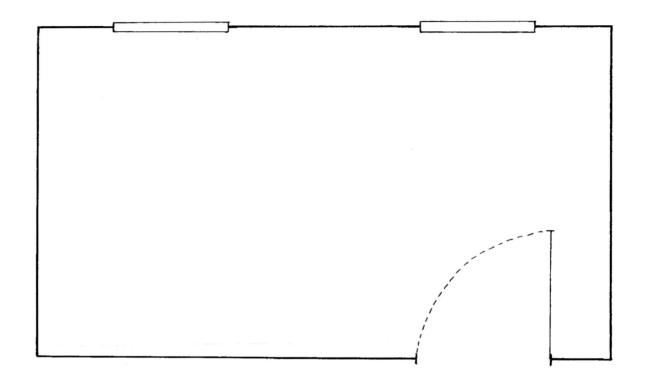

Corta los muebles y ponlos en el plano.

Cut out the furniture and put it on the plan.

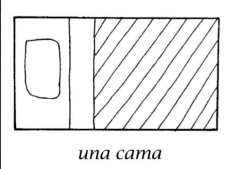

una cama

una silla

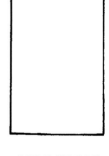

una mesa

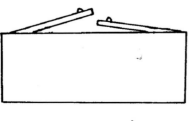

un armario

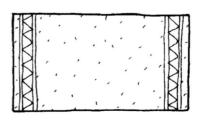

una alfombra

¡Es Español! © Kathy Williams and Beatriz Rubio

Learning objectives

Pupils will be able to:
* Say the months of the year
* Say when their birthday is
* Recognize some special festival days and names and find out about their significance
* Say how old they are
* Use numbers to 31

Resources needed.

* Sheets 8a, 8b, 8c, 8d; CD Tracks 10–12
* Pictures from magazines/ photographs/book illustrations showing different weather conditions; glitter; glue; card/ paper.

Activities

* Using a variety of weather pictures (or sheet 4a flashcards) elicit suitable months for each (in Spanish if possible, or English to start).

* Listen and practise pronunciation of the months. Pupils match illustrations with names of months on sheet 8a.

* Pupils suggest months for various activities 'holidays?', 'skiing?', 'New Year', 'at school?', etc.

* The question: '¿Cuándo es tu cumpleanõs?' is introduced on the CD. Pupils say which month their birthday is in, eg 'Es en marzo'. Highlight 'es' and 'en'.

* Revise numbers to 20 (Unit 5). Continue with the numbers 21 to 31. Pupils use the appropriate

Vocabulario – Key words

enero	January
febrero	February
marzo	March
abril	April
mayo	May
junio	June
julio	July
agosto	August
septiembre	September
octubre	October
noviembre	November
diciembre	December
los mesos del año	the months of the year
una fiesta	a celebration
Navidad	Christmas
Semana Santa	Easter
Nochebuena	Christmas Eve
el doce de octubre	12th October
es	it is
en	in
¿cuántos años tienes?	how old are you?
tengo … años	I'm … years old
Feliz Navidad	Merry Xmas
Feliz Año	Happy New Year
Feliz Cumpleaños	Happy Birthday
mi cumpleaños	my birthday
el día de la madre	Mother's day
los números 21–31	
veintiuno	twenty-one
veintidós	twenty-two
veintitrés	twenty-three
veinticuatro	twenty-four
veinticinco	twenty-five
veintiséis	twenty-six
veintisiete	twenty-seven
veintiocho	twenty-eight
veintinueve	twenty-nine
treinta	thirty
treinta y uno	thirty-one

number to say when the date of their birthday is, eg 'Es el diecisiete de febrero.'

✳ Introduce how to say age: 'Tengo ... años'. Pupils say how old they are in response to the question '¿Cuántos años tienes?' Pupils can complete sheet 8b for reinforcement.

✳ 👂 Sheet 8b (CD Track 11). Sing 'Happy Birthday to you' in Spanish.

✳ Prepare a set of cards/papers which have either nothing or 'hoy' (today) written on them. Ask pupils to choose a card. If they pick a blank card move to the next pupil. The pupil who chooses an 'hoy' card says 'Es mi cumpleaños.' (The rest of the class could sing 'Happy Birthday in Spanish.) The pupil makes up how old he/she is and says this in Spanish.

✳ Talk about Christmas and other celebrations in Spain. Pupils could find out more about other special occasions in Spain (see Background information in Appendix for information on some other festivals celebrated in Spain).

✳ Pupils could make Christmas/Mother's Day cards with greetings in Spanish.

✳ Use the wordsearch on sheet 8c to practise and revise the months, celebrations, days and seasons.

✳ 👂 On Sheet 8d pupils need to work out which words match which pictures. Listen to the CD for the correct pronunciation of the items: un reno = a reindeer; un árbol de Navidad = a Christmas tree; un muñeco de nieve = a snowman; una estrella = a star; Papá Noel = Father Christmas; un regalo = a present. The phrase for snowman (muñeco de nieve) is literally 'snow doll'. The word is also used to refer to dolls in general (muñeca for a female doll).

Further activities

✳ Pupils could find out the birthdays of famous people and report them to the group.

✳ They could write their own wordsearch containing months/celebrations. They could put these into Christmas cards for friends in the group or other friends/family.

✳ Pupils could cut potato prints in the shape of a Christmas tree, snowman, star, present, etc to make a Christmas card/poster/wrapping/tree decoration.

Los meses del año

The months of the year

Une los meses con los dibujos.

Match the months with the pictures.

enero	agosto	junio	diciembre
febrero	septiembre	abril	octubre
noviembre	marzo	julio	mayo

¿Cuándo es tu cumpleaños?

When is your birthday?

¡Es mi cumpleaños!

Copia las frases.
Copy the sentences.

Es en febrero.

_____ ___ _____.

Es el diecisiete de febrero.

____ ___ _____ _____.

Canta esta canción.
Sing this song.

Cumpleaños feliz
Cumpleaños feliz
Te deseamos todos
Cumpleaños feliz.

Cumpleaños feliz
Te deseamos a ti
Y que por muchos años
Tú los puedas cumplir.

Tengo <u>diez</u> años.
¿Cuántos años tienes?

_____ ____ ____.

¡Es Español!   © Kathy Williams and Beatriz Rubio

Las fiestas, los meses, los días y las estaciones

Celebrations, months, days and seasons

Las palabras están escondidas en la sopa de letras.

The words are all hidden in the wordsearch.

S	M	A	Y	O	Q	D	I	C	I	E	M	B	R	E
E	I	C	E	S	T	A	C	I	O	N	M	U	X	Y
P	E	N	O	V	I	E	M	B	R	E	A	J	J	C
T	R	A	D	O	M	I	N	G	O	R	R	U	U	S
I	C	V	I	E	R	N	E	S	S	O	Z	L	E	E
E	O	I	N	F	E	B	R	E	R	O	O	I	V	M
M	L	D	V	J	M	A	R	T	E	S	R	O	E	A
B	E	A	I	U	L	U	N	E	S	R	P	C	S	N
R	S	D	E	N	H	M	F	A	G	O	S	T	O	A
E	B	T	R	I	A	B	R	I	L	Q	A	U	T	S
G	L	P	N	O	V	E	R	A	N	O	B	B	O	A
M	E	S	O	F	I	E	S	T	A	Ñ	A	R	Ñ	N
P	R	I	M	A	V	E	R	A	J	L	D	E	O	T
C	U	M	P	L	E	A	Ñ	O	S	V	O	D	I	A

mes	cumpleaños	estación
Navidad	lunes	enero
jueves	febrero	diciembre
martes	verano	domingo
julio	marzo	junio
fiesta	septiembre	agosto
noviembre	Semana Santa	primavera
abril	mayo	miércoles
viernes	otoño	sábado
invierno	octubre	día

¡Es Español!
www.brilliantpublications.co.uk

¡Es Navidad!

It's Christmas!

¿Qué es?
What is it?

Un reno

Un árbol de Navidad   **Christmas tree**

Un muñeco de nieve

Una estrella

Papá Noel

Un regalo

¡Es Español!   © Kathy Williams and Beatriz Rubio

Países del mundo

Learning objectives

Pupils will be able to:

✱   Name some countries and nationalities
✱   Say their own nationality
✱   Name the colours of some flags

Resources needed

✱   Sheet 9a, 9b, 9c; Track 13.
✱   Dice; flags or flag pictures; bag; selection of small coloured items; books and other sources of information on countries; maps.

Activities

✱ 🎧   Some European countries are introduced on the CD. Pupils identify countries on the map (sheet 9a) by drawing lines from the countries to the children. Fill in the missing country names together.

✱   Assign one of the people names from sheet 9a to each pupil. Go round the group at random. The pupils introduce themselves using that name and 'Vivo en ...'. Highlight use of 'en'. Alternatively pupils could say where they actually live.

✱   Number the countries on sheet 9a. Playing in pairs or small groups, invite pupils to roll a dice naming the corresponding country and adding the score in Spanish.

✱ 🎧   Listen to the nationalities introduced on the CD. Pupils decide who, from sheet 9a, is talking.

✱ 🎧   Highlight masculine and feminine for inglés/inglesa, irlandés/irlandesa, escocés/escocesa, francés/francesa, galés/galesa. Look at the masculine/

Vocabulario – Key words

vivo en	I live in
Inglaterra	England
Escocia	Scotland
Irlanda del Norte	Northern Ireland
el País de Gales	Wales
España	Spain
Alemania	Germany
Francia	France
Italia	Italy
Irlanda	Ireland
soy	I am
inglés(esa)	English
español(esa)	Spanish
irlandés(esa)	Irish
escocés(esa)	Scottish
galés(esa)	Welsh
alemán(ana)	German
francés(esa)	French
italiano/a	Italian
¿de qué color es?	what colour is?
la bandera de …	the flag of …
rojo/a	red
azul	blue
amarillo/a	yellow
rosa	pink
negro/a	black
violeta	purple
verde	green
blanco/a	white
naranja	orange
marrón	brown

See Units 10 and 11 for other colours.

feminine forms of another three nationalities: alemán/alemana, español/española, italiano/italiana. An explanation of this appears on the CD.

✱ Go round the group asking pupils to say where they live and their nationality. Highlight 'Soy ...'.

✱ 👂 Using flags/flag pictures/pupils' knowledge ask '¿De qué color es la bandera española?' 'Es roja, amarilla y roja.' Follow with 'la bandera italiana', then 'la bandera alemana' (colours are on the CD and are listed in Vocabulario). Use sheet 9b for reinforcement: pupils could colour the flags. Highlight the fact that 'bandera' in Spanish is feminine; therefore when accompanied by colours these have to agree in gender – 'La bandera española es roja, amarilla y roja.' See Vocabulario to check which colours take feminine form: eg rojo/a, amarillo/a, negro/a, blanco/a. Azul, violeta, verde, naranja and marrón do not take a feminine form.

✱ Give pupils a selection of coloured items. They state the colour and place the item into a bag. When you have collected all the items ask pupils, eg '¿De qué color es el balón?' They must guess/remember the colour. You take that item out of the bag and the pupils either agree, eg 'Sí, es verde' or disagree 'No, es azul.'

✱ Ask pupils to close their eyes and hand them each an item that they have previously seen. Without opening their eyes they say the colour of the item from memory. They then check and correct themselves if necessary.

✱ Sheet 9c provides reading comprehension, tests colours and introduces opinions.

✱ Extend work on countries and flags. A 'Países diferentes' (Different countries) display could be made. Pupils could choose a country and find out further information about it, including the design/colours of its flag.

Further activities
✱ Pupils all stand up holding their coloured item. You or another pupil call out a colour drawn from a bag. All those with an item of that colour sit down. The winner(s) is the person left standing the longest.

✱ Hide coloured objects around the classroom/hall, etc. When you say a colour pupils must find an object of that colour within a time limit (or while you play a music CD) and return to their places with it, or touch it when the music stops. Those with no coloured object or the incorrect colour are out of the game. Plan the game so that there will only be one or two of the last coloured items to find. Players still in the game at the end are the winners.

✱ Pupils could find out more about Spanish–speaking countries around the world.

¡Es Español! © Kathy Williams and Beatriz Rubio

Vivo en ...

I live in ...

🦻 **Escucha y une los dibujos de las personas con sus países.**
Listen and match the pictures of the people with their countries.

Me llamo Dieter.
Vivo en _____.

Me llamo Claudette.
Vivo en _____.

Me llamo Gordon.
Vivo en _____.

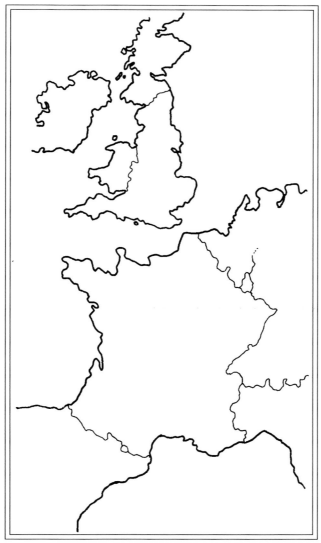

Me llamo Emilio.
Vivo en _____.

Me llamo Jane.
Vivo en _____.

Me llamo David.
Vivo en _____.

Me llamo Bernadette.
Vivo en _____.

Me llamo Carmen.
Vivo en _____.

© **Kathy Williams and Beatriz Rubio**   **¡Es Español!**   47

www.brilliantpublications.co.uk

¿De qué color es la bandera española?

What colour is the Spanish flag?

Hola, me llamo _____.

Vivo _____.

Soy _____.

La bandera es _____.

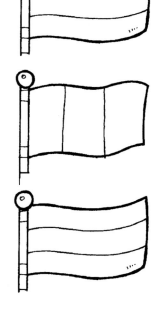

La bandera española es roja, amarilla y roja.

La bandera italiana es verde, blanca y roja.

La bandera alemana es negra, roja y amarilla.

¿Hay una bandera violeta? Sí, la bandera de Chad en África es violeta, amarilla y roja.

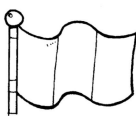

¡Es Español!   © Kathy Williams and Beatriz Rubio

Hablando de colores

Talking about colours

Lee el texto y contesta a las preguntas en inglés:

Read this passage and answer the questions in English:

Miguel: ¿Cuál es tu color preferido, Marcos?

Marcos: El azul. Prefiero el azul.

Miguel: ¿Y el tuyo, Sofía?

Sofía: Es … el rosa, y también el amarillo.

Miguel: ¿Y el tuyo, Francisco?

Francisco: ¡Qué difícil! Me gusta el violeta y el verde también.

Miguel: ¿Cuál es tu color preferido, Manuel?

Manuel: A mí me gusta el amarillo. Y no me gusta el gris.

Miguel: Y a mí me gusta el azul, pero como Manuel prefiero el amarillo.

1. What question is Miguel asking all his friends? _____
    _____

2. What does Marcos reply? _____

3. What about Sofía? _____

4. Why does Francisco say it is a difficult question? _____

5. What does Manuel say? _____

6. Which colour(s) are the most popular? _____

Encuentra los colores. Puedes colorearlos.

Find the colours. You can colour them in.

naranja
azul
verde
blanco
rojo
amarillo
negro
violeta
rosa
marrón

V	M	A	R	R	O	N	D	B	J
I	P	Z	O	E	V	E	R	D	E
O	T	U	S	C	U	G	M	F	L
L	C	L	A	T	L	R	O	J	O
E	B	L	A	N	C	O	E	G	N
T	N	A	R	A	N	J	A	H	R
A	M	A	R	I	L	L	O	I	S

¿Te gustan los animales?

Learning objectives

Pupils will be able to:
* Name some animals and say if they have one
* Give simple descriptions of animals
* Express opinions
* Understand construction of plurals

Resources needed
* Sheets 10a, 10b, 10c, 10d, 10e; CD Tracks 14–15.
* Different fruit (optional); sticky labels; animal models/toys.

Activities

* Introduce animal words (pets) with flashcards sheet 10a. All are masculine except spider.

* Place the animal cards face down. A pupil chooses one. Without looking he/she takes a guess 'Es un/una …,' checks and class agrees or corrects 'Sí, es …' or 'No, es …' The winner is the first person to guess correctly.

* Sheet 10b is a vocabulary matching exercise. Introduce '¿Qué es?' (What is it?).

* Use the CD to introduce the question '¿Te gustan los animales?' and the responses 'Sí, me gustan los animales/No, no me gustan los animales.' Go round the group asking pupils for responses.

* Use flashcards (sheet 10a) to focus on creating questions similar to those on sheet 10c, Elicit replies from the group.

* Sheet 10c. Pupils survey a selection of classmates and record their replies in Spanish. The spoken replies must be in full sentences using 'Sí, me gustan los/las …'/No, no me gustan los/las …'. Highlight 'los' as the plural form of 'the' in the masculine form and 'las' in the feminine form, eg 'las arañas'. Highlight the 's' of plural nouns which finish in a vowel, such as 'perro' (dog),

Vocabulario – Key words

los animales	animals
los animales domésticos	
	pets
¿qué es?	what is it?
un gato	a cat
un perro	a dog
un caballo	a horse
un conejo	a rabbit
un pájaro	a bird
un conejo de Indias	a guinea pig
un pez	a fish
un ratón	a mouse
una araña	a spider
naranja	orange
blanco/a	white
marrón	brown
gris	grey
¿te gusta/n …?	do you like …?
me gusta/n …	I like …
no me gusta/n …	I don't like …
tengo ...	I have ...
es …	he/she/it is …
pequeño/a	small
grande	big
lindo	cute

¡Es Español! © Kathy Williams and Beatriz Rubio

'araña' (spider), etc. Indicate the use of 'es' to make the plural of nouns which finish in a consonant like 'ratón' (mouse) and 'pez' (fish) where another change applies. The 'z' changes into a 'c' and then 'es' is added. (See Appendix for formation of plurals.)

✷ 🎧 Listen to and practise the question '¿Tienes animales?' and the reply 'Sí, tengo un perro.' Pupils could reply with own animals. (You may need a dictionary to look up further words.) Alternatively pupils could each have an animal flashcard (sheet 10a) and say 'Tengo, un/una …'.

✷ Write the names of animals on sticky labels. Stick one on the back of each pupil, without letting them read the labels first. Each pupil must discover what pet he/she has by asking '¿Tengo un/una …?' to another pupil, who replies simply with 'Sí' or 'No'. Everyone continues asking, to a different classmate each time, until they have discovered what animal name is on their back.

✷ 🎧 Sheet 10d. Pupils listen to the descriptions on the CD and identify the correct animals. This exercise uses colours from Unit 9, plus some other adjectives. The phrases at the bottom of the sheet highlight 'Es …' 'He/she/it is …'. Highlight use of 'este' (this is) in masculine form. (See Unit 10 and Appendix.)

✷ Pupils can be encouraged to describe their own pets and draw them (could be used for display).

✷ 🎧 Sheet 10e (CD Track 15). Song: 'Debajo de un botón'. This song is about a very small mouse ('chiquitín') that was found under a button. Pupils can sing along with the CD. Note: the 'de' in the title is not pronounced when the song is sung.

Further activities

✷ Pupils mime or make animal noises for their partner to guess 'Es un/una …'.

✷ Follow up the survey (sheet 10c) by drawing a graph/pie chart to show popularity of animals. 'El más popular es el/la …'.

✷ Provide a selection of fruit for pupils to taste (some are named on sheet 10c). Pupils record opinions using 'Me gusta' or 'No, no me gusta.'

✷ Encourage pupils to use dictionaries to prepare further surveys on other topics (see Appendix for note on use of singular/plural in the question '¿Te gusta/n el/la/los/las?'

Los animales domésticos (flashcards)

¡Es Español! © Kathy Williams and Beatriz Rubio

Los animales domésticos

Pets

¿Qué es?

What is it?

un perro   un gato   un caballo
un conejo   una araña   un conejo de Indias
un pez   un ratón   un pájaro

Es un gato.

Es _____.

Es _____.

Es _____.

Es _____.

Es _____.

Es _____.

Es _____.

Es _____.

¿Te gustan los animales?

Do you like animals?

Una encuesta

A survey

Pregunta a tus amigos.

Ask your friends.

Escribe 'Sí' o 'No'.

¿Te gustan …	Sí	No
los perros?		
los peces?		
los gatos?		
las arañas?		
los ratones?		
los pájaros?		
los caballos?		

¿Qué animal es el más popular? _____

Fruta

¿Te gustan …   eg   Sí, me gustan las manzanas.

No, no me gustan las manzanas.

Las manzanas?   _____

Los plátanos?   _____

Las peras?   _____

Las fresas?   _____

Los kiwis?   _____

¡Es Español!   © Kathy Williams and Beatriz Rubio

Es pequeño y naranja ...

He is small and orange ...

Escucha las descripciones. ¿Qué animal es? Escribe el número.

Listen to the descriptions. Which animal is it? Write the number.

Lee las frases.

Read the sentences.

Éste es mi hamster. Es pequeño y lindo. Es marrón.

Éste es mi perro. Es grande y negro.

Éste es mi ratón. Es lindo. Es blanco.

Debajo de un botón

Under a button

Canta esta canción.

Sing this song.

Debajo un botón, ton, ton del Señor Martín, tin, tin
Había un ratón, ton, ton, !ay, qué chiquitín, tin, tin!
!ay, qué chíquitín, tin, tin era aquel ratón ton, ton
que encontró Martín, tin, tin, debajo un botón, ton, ton!

Es tan juguetón, ton, ton, el Señor Martín, tin, tin
Que metió al ratón ton ton, en un calcetín, tin, tin
En un calcetín, tin tin vive aquel ratón ton ton
Lo metió Martín tin tin porque es juguetón ton ton.

(Otra vez, pero más rápido.)

(Again, but faster.)

¡Es Español! © *Kathy Williams and Beatriz Rubio*

Mi familia

Learning objectives

✳ **Pupils will be able to:**

✳ Describe who is in their family or who someone is

✳ Use mi (possessive) and the demonstrative este/esta

✳ Use hair and eye colour descriptions for self and others

Resources needed

✳ Sheets 11a, 11b, 11c, 11d, 11e; CD Tracks 16–17.

✳ Family photographs; dolls; puppets.

Activities

✳ 👂 Introduce 'Ésta es mi familia', 'Éste es mi padre' and 'Ésta es mi madre.'

✳ 👂 Revise 'Me llamo …'

✳ On sheet 11a ask pupils to draw 'father' and 'mother' faces onto the seaside pictures. Cut the sheets into four. The pupils then pick a card at random and show it to the group saying either 'Éste es mi padre' or 'Ésta es mi madre.' Highlight the possessive, 'mi', and the demonstrative 'este', 'esta' (see Appendix).

✳ 👂 Listen to the question: '¿Tienes hermanos?' Note that in Spanish the masculine plural form tends to be inclusive; therefore the meaning of this question is: 'have you got brothers and sisters?' Pupils follow the model given on the CD to describe whether they have brothers or sisters using 'Tengo …'. Give the phrase 'No tengo' for pupils who have no brothers or sisters.

✳ Sheet 11b. In exercise 1 pupils need to draw lines to link the children on the left with their brothers/sisters on the right and write appropriate sentences. This exercise revises numbers one to five (see Unit 5).

✳ 👂 Listen and practise the question: '¿Quién es?' On sheet 11b, exercise 2, pupils look at the pictures (for exercises 1 and 2) and complete the sentences.

✳ Distribute family group cards (sheet 11c), one per pupil. There are 30 cards in total, divided into 10 horizontal family groups of 3. (If you have less pupils

Vocabulario – Key words

éste/ésta es …	this is …
mi	my
mi madre	my mother
mi padre	my father
un hermano	a (one) brother
una hermana	a sister
tengo	I have
no tengo	I haven't any
¿quién es?	who is it?
el pelo	hair
los ojos	eyes
marrón(ones)	brown/chestnut
rojo	red/ginger
negro(s)	black
moreno	brown (hair)
azul(es)	blue
verde(s)	green
tiene …	he has …/she has …

divide the cards appropriately. For example, if you have 10 pupils, use 2 x sets of 3 and 2 x sets of 2. For 20 pupils use 6 x sets of 3 and 1 x set of 2, etc. For sets of 2, white out the names that don't apply.) Pupils circulate around the class saying 'Hola, me llamo …' then, for example, 'Tengo un hermano, Pablo y una hermana María.' If the person they are talking to matches the family group by being Pedro or María, they introduce themselves and then go as a pair in search of their missing third person. When all the family sets are complete the pupils could introduce themselves.

✱ Using family photographs, pupils explain who is who on the picture using 'Es mi hermano/Es mi hermana', etc in pairs or to the group.

✱ ☉ Listen to the poem: 'Tengo los ojos marrones', which uses eye and hair colours (see sheet 11d). Ask pupils to identify the colours. Clap to the rhythm of the poem. As a group pupils could join in the whole poem, then repeat it with the pupils chanting only those parts that apply to them. Point to hair and eyes as the poem progresses. Highlight that 'los ojos' is plural; therefore the adjective will have to be in plural as well. However, 'el pelo' is singular and so will be the adjective.

✱ Pupils describe own hair and eyes using 'Tengo el pelo …/Tengo los ojos…'.

✱ Use dolls, puppets, etc to reinforce 'Tiene el pelo … moreno' and 'Tiene los ojos … azules', etc. Pupils could colour in each of the four hair/eye colours on the four people on sheet 11a. They could then describe to a partner the colours they have given to their characters' hair and eyes. They could colour further pictures with funny hair/eye colour choices.

✱ Pupils describe their own family members. Sheet 11d provides further reinforcement: pupils draw and describe themselves and a family member.

✱ ☉ Sheet 11e (CD Track 17). Song: 'José se llamaba el padre'. Highlight that people's names also take masculine and feminine forms. All women's names in this song finish in 'a' as most feminine common names do.

Further activities

✱ Pupils could draw a family picture and write descriptions to match using the language in this unit.

✱ Work in pairs. Pupils study each other's family photographs then hide them from view. Pupils take it in turns to describe each other's relatives using, eg 'Tiene los ojos marrones ...' when prompted by 'mi hermano/mi padre', etc.

✱ Pupils describe a class member and others guess the person.

Éste es mi padre, ésta es mi madre

This is my dad, this is my mum

¿Tienes hermanos?

Do you have any brothers and sisters?

Ejercicio 1 **Une cada persona con su familia.**
Match each person with their family.

Tengo un hermano y una hermana .

_____

_____

_____

_____

Ejercicio 2 **¿Quién es?**
Who is it?

1   ?   Es mi hermano.

2   ?   Es _____ .

3   ?   Es _____ .

4   ?    Es mi _____ .

¡Es Español!   © Kathy Williams and Beatriz Rubio

Hermanos y hermanas

Brothers and sisters

1 hermano Pablo **Marcos** 1 hermana María	1 hermano Marcos **Pablo** 1 hermana María	1 hermano Marcos **María** 1 hermano Pablo
1 hermano Miguel **Tomás** 1 hermana Lucía	1 hermano Tomás **Miguel** 1 hermana Lucía	1 hermano Tomás **Lucía** 1 hermano Miguel
1 hermano Andrés **Lucas** 1 hermana Inés	1 hermano Lucas **Andrés** 1 hermana Inés	1 hermano Lucas **Inés** 1 hermano Andrés
1 hermano Daniel **Sebastián** 1 hermana Coral	1 hermano Sebastián **Daniel** 1 hermana Coral	1 hermano Sebastián **Coral** 1 hermano Daniel
1 hermano David **Claudio** 1 hermana Elena	1 hermano Claudio **David** 1 hermana Elena	1 hermano Claudio **Elena** 1 hermano David
1 hermano Alberto **Felipe** 1 hermana Ángela	1 hermano Felipe **Alberto** 1 hermana Ángela	1 hermano Alberto **Angela** 1 hermano Felipe
1 hermano Juan **Cristóbal** 1 hermana Miriam	1 hermano Cristóbal **Juan** 1 hermana Miriam	1 hermano Cristóbal **Miriam** 1 hermano Juan
1 hermano Manuel **Pedro** 1 hermana Pilar	1 hermano Pedro **Manuel** 1 hermana Pilar	1 hermano Pedro **Pilar** 1 hermano Manuel
1 hermana Susana **Elisa** 1 hermana Leticia	1 hermana Elisa **Susana** 1 hermana Leticia	1 hermana Elisa **Leticia** 1 hermana Susana
1 hermana Cristina **Sofía** 1 hermana Mónica	1 hermana Sofía **Cristina** 1 hermana Mónica	1 hermana Sofía **Mónica** 1 hermana Cristina

Tengo los ojos marrones

I've got brown eyes

Tengo los ojos marrones, marrones.
Tengo los ojos azules, azules.
Tengo los ojos verdes, verdes.
Tengo los ojos negros, negros.

Tengo el pelo moreno, moreno.
Tengo el pelo rojo, rojo.
Tengo el pelo rubio, rubio.
Tengo el pelo negro, negro.

Completa las frases.

Complete the sentences.

Soy yo. _____.

Tengo el pelo _____.

Tengo los ojos _____.

Es _____.

Tiene el pelo _____.

Tiene los ojos _____.

Tiene …
He has …

Tiene …
She has …

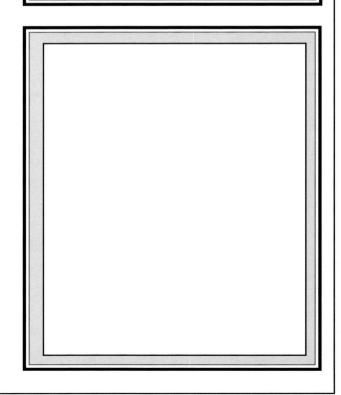

¡Es Español!   © Kathy Williams and Beatriz Rubio

José se llamaba el padre

José was the name of the father

Canta esta canción.

Sing this song.

José se llamaba el padre,
Josefa la mujer
Y tenían un hijito que se llamaba …

José se llamaba el padre,
Josefa la mujer
Y tenían un hijito que se llamaba.

Manuel se llamaba el padre,
Manuela la mujer,
Y tenían un hijito que se llamaba …

(otra vez)
(again)

Ramón se llamaba el padre,
Ramona la mujer,
Y tenían un hijito que se llamaba …

(otra vez)
(again)

Fermín se llamaba el padre,
Fermina la mujer,
Y tenían un hijito que se llamaba …

(otra vez)
(again)

¡Es Español!

www.brilliantpublications.co.uk

De vacaciones

Learning objectives

Pupils will be able to:

* Say where they are going using 'voy'
* Use some destinations using 'a/al'
* Talk about modes of transport using 'en' and 'a'
* Ask where someone is going

Resources needed

* Sheets 12a, 12b, 12c, 12d; CD Track 18.
* Map; ribbon/string; magazine travel pictures; travel brochures.

Activities

* Introduce the question ¿Dónde vas ...? and three holiday areas (beach/country/mountains) using 'Voy a'. Note that as countryside in Spanish is masuline 'el campo' with the preposition 'a' becomes 'al' (a+el): 'Voy al campo'. Use flashcards (sheet 12a) to aid comprehension. Pupils choose a destination they would prefer using 'Voy a/al ...'.

Vocabulario – Key words

¿dónde vas?	where are you going?
voy ...	I am going ...
a la playa	to the beach
al campo	to the countryside
a la montaña	to the mountains
a Francia	to France
a Escocia	to Scotland
a Irlanda	to Ireland
a Londres	to London
a Cardiff	to Cardiff
¡buen viaje!	Have a good trip!
un/en avión	a/by plane
un/en barco	a/by boat
un/en autobús	a/by bus
un/en coche	a/by car
una/en bicicleta	a/by bike
un/en tren	a/by train
un/a pie	a/on foot
un/a caballo	a/on horse(back)

* Introduce the use of 'voy a' + town.

* Explain that when we are going to a country we use 'Voy a'. Ask pupils to suggest their own destinations using 'Voy a la playa', etc and a country name (see Unit 9 for country names).

* Sheet 12b reinforces the use of 'Voy a/al'.

* Introduce modes of transport using the flashcards on sheet 12c and the CD.

* Use flashcards (sheet 12c). Hold them up and ask the pupils to select one form of transport. Turn the cards over then ask several pupils to pick one card each, without looking at the pictures. The one who has chosen the form of transport that the class decided on earlier is the one who is 'going on holiday'. He/she says, eg 'Soy yo. Voy a París' and adds on the form of transport, eg 'en avión'. Everyone else says '¡Buen viaje!' and the game continues until everyone is 'de vacaciones'.

¡Es Español! © *Kathy Williams and Beatriz Rubio*

✷ Sheet 12d. Give each pupil a copy of sheet 12d. They play in pairs. Each pupil hides their grid from their partner and places the seven forms of transport in his/her grid using pictures (and words if wished). Player 1 reads out a numbered grid reference in Spanish. If their partner has a picture in that square he/she says 'Sí'. Player 1 then guesses the transport word. If they are right the picture is crossed off and Player 1 continues. If wrong, Player 2 has a turn and Player 1 must wait his/her turn to guess another form of transport for that box. The winner is the player to guess all his/her opponents' positions and transport correctly. Encourage pupils to use 'un/una' correctly. All the transport words introduced here are masculine except 'una bicicleta'.

✷ 🜂 Pupils use question '¿Dónde vas?' to ask each other where they are going 'de vacaciones' for the next approaching holiday period. Pupils can try to explain as far as possible where, how and when they are going (for dates refer to Unit 8).

✷ Use cut-up travel brochures or magazine pictures for pupils to invent future travel plans/itineraries.

Further activities

✷ Pupils could research the AVE train services in Spain.

✷ Using a map, pupils could mark places to be visited in the holidays and connect these to 'home' with a ribbon, string or drawn line. They could write short descriptions of how their places are to be reached, eg 'Voy a Francia en avión.' Pupils could make small transport symbols, labelled in Spanish, to attach to the connecting line.

✷ A transport frieze could be made around the room.

De vacaciones

On holiday (flashcards)

¡Es Español!   © *Kathy Williams and Beatriz Rubio*

¿Dónde vas de vacaciones?

Where are you going on holiday?

Ejercicio 1　　　**Une los animales con sus destinos:**

Match the animals with their destinations:

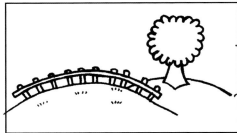　　al campo　　　a la playa　　　a la montaña

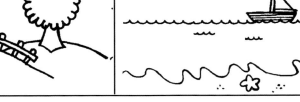

Ejercicio 2

Voy ...

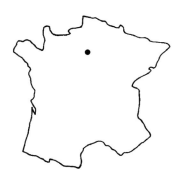

... a París

... a Francia

... a Roma

... a Italia

¿Dónde van Pierre y Gianni?　　Pierre:　Voy _____

Gianni:　Voy _____

Medios de transporte (flashcards)

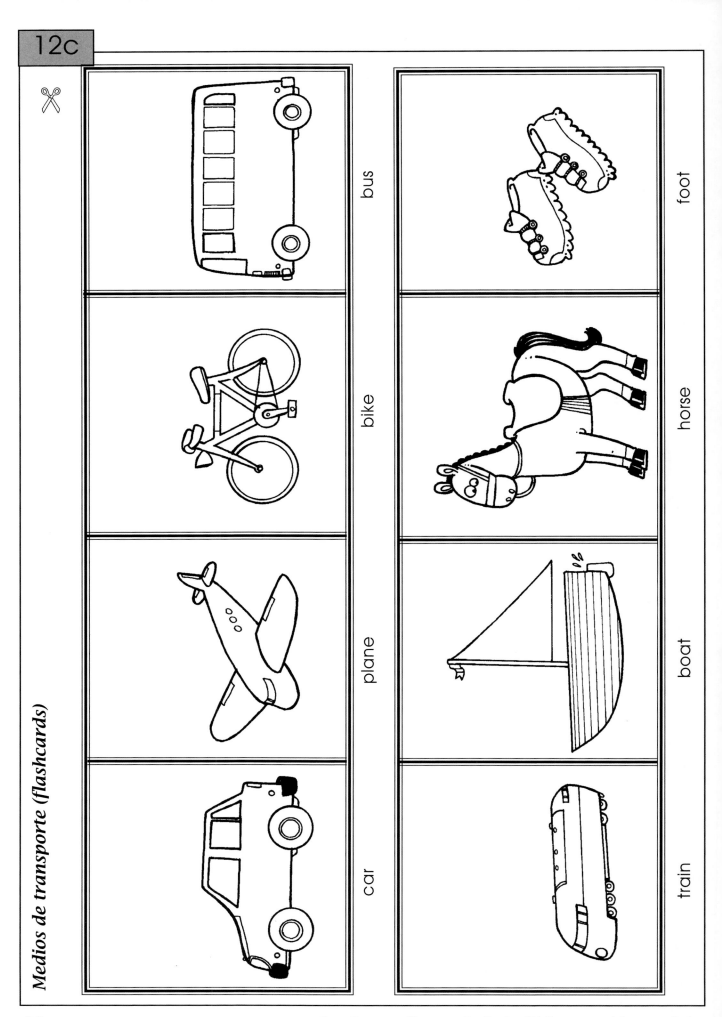

bus

foot

bike

horse

plane

boat

car

train

¡Es Español!

El juego de transporte

The transport game

una bicicleta

un coche

un autobús

4

3

2

1

A   B   C

un pie

Dibuja siete medios de transporte en el gráfico; tú decides dónde. Quedarán cinco casillas vacías.

Draw seven modes of transport in the grid;
you decide where. There will be five empty boxes.

un avión

un barco

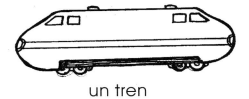

un tren

Mi día

Learning objectives

Pupils will be able to:

✱ Describe some activities using regular verbs and irregular verbs

✱ Say what the time is, on the hour

✱ Talk about school subjects they like/don't like

✱ Describe the school day

Resources needed

✱ Sheets 13a, 13b, 13c, 13d, 13e; CD Track 19.

✱ Pupils' school timetable; clock faces.

Activities

✱ 🕮 Weather expressions (fine, bad, snowing, raining) revised from Unit 4. There are pauses on the CD to allow the pupils to answer.

✱ 🕮 Listen to the CD: 'Cuando hace bueno/llueve', etc. Pupils pick a picture (from sheet 13a) to go with each weather expression they hear. Highlight 'cuando' (when). In English, discuss what activities you could do 'Cuando hace malo/hace sol', etc (Spanish verbs are introduced in the next activity).

✱ 🕮 Listen to the activity phrases on the CD. Encourage pupils to complete the weather sentences with an appropriate activity phrase in Spanish.

✱ Sheet 13b. Pupils repeat the exercise by drawing lines to match weather and activity choices.

✱ 🕮 Sheet 13c shows daily 'routine' activities. Give each pupil a strip and ask them to cut it up and mix

Vocabulario – Key words

¿cuándo?	when?
mi tiempo libre	my free time
juego	I play
veo	I watch
me quedo	I stay
como	I eat
hablo	I talk
llego	I arrive
trabajo	I work
vuelvo	I return
escucho	I listen
un compañero	a mate/pal
es la una	it is one o'clock
son las ...	it is ...
a la/las ...	at ... o'clock
mi horario	my timetable
las matemáticas	maths
las ciencias	science
la educación física	sport
el dibujo	art
el inglés	English
la lengua española	Spanish
la música	music
la historia	history
la geografía	geography
la informática	ICT/computers
divertido	fun
interesante	interesting
aburrido	boring
bastante difícil	quite difficult
genial	super

For weather expressions see Unit 4.

¡Es Español!   © Kathy Williams and Beatriz Rubio

up the pieces. They then listen to the CD and arrange the pictures in what they feel is the correct order. Discuss the phrases and the order in pairs/ group. Highlight the end 'o' for the first person singular.

✱ Sheet 13d: pupils stick pictures (from sheet 13c) in the correct order and fill in the verbs. Highlight how all the verbs end in 'o'.

✱ 👂 Look at sheet 13d. Agree with the pupils when each of the activities might take place (to the nearest hour). Display clock faces for the agreed times in a prominent position. Listen to the CD to introduce 'son las …/es la ...'. Mime activities. Pupils have to give an appropriate time. For example, if you mime eating breakfast they might say 'Son las siete'.

✱ Repeat the above activity, but this time give a time, eg 'Son las nueve'. The pupils might respond 'Llego a la escuela'. They could practise this in pairs as well.

✱ Sheet 13d, exercise 2. Pupils match the times on the clocks with the phrases, writing the corresponding number in the boxes beneath the clocks.

✱ 👂 Introduce school subjects. Using sheet 13e, pupils listen to the CD and try to identify which day is being referred to. Pupils could pretend to be Javier and make up phrases about the school day, based on his timetable, eg 'A ... tengo' + subject.

✱ Pupils can create their own sentences and phrases using their own school timetable.

✱ 👂 Introduce adjectives to describe school subjects. Pupils express opinions about school subjects and fill in sheet 13e, exercise 2.

Further activities

✱ Practise times by pinning clock faces round the room showing different times. Pupils point to or collect the correct clock to show understanding. Pupils could work in pairs to test each other.

✱ Pupils could find out more about Spanish school customs and the school day in Spain. They could compare their subject areas with those from Spain. You could discuss how English would be the equivalent 'foreign language' for Spanish children.

✱ Pupils could draw up a bar chart of preferred/least liked subjects labelled in Spanish.

El tiempo (flashcards)

¡Es Español!   © Kathy Williams and Beatriz Rubio

Mi tiempo libre

My free time

Une cada actividad con el tiempo que hace:
Match an activity with the weather at the time:

Cuando hace bueno …

juego en el parque.

Cuando nieva …

veo la televisión.

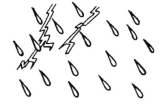

Cuando hace malo …

juego en el parque.

Cuando llueve …

me quedo en casa.

Cuando hace calor …

juego en el jardín.

La rutina diaria (flashcards)

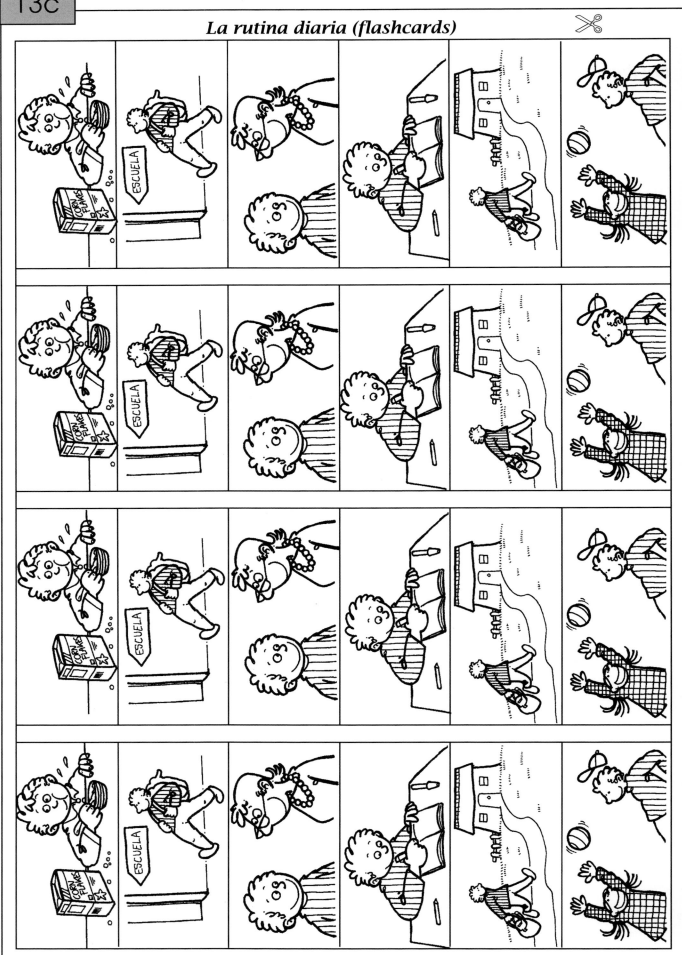

¡Es Español! © Kathy Williams and Beatriz Rubio

Mi día en la escuela

My day at school

Rellena los espacios:

Fill in the blanks:

Ejercicio 1

_____ mi desayuno

_____ a la escuela.

_____ al profesor.

_____ en clase.

_____ a casa.

_____ con mis compañeros.

vuelvo

juego

como

escucho

llego

trabajo

Ejercicio 2   Escribe el número correcto:

Write in the correct number:

1.   Son las diez.
2.   Son las siete.
3.   Son las cuatro.
4.   Son las nueve.

Mi horario

My timetable

Ejercicio 1 **Escucha y decide qué día es.**
Listen and decide which day it is.

Éste es mi horario de clase.

Javier

	9h	10h	11h	12h	1h–2h	4h
lunes	las matemáticas		las ciencias		la educación física	
martes	el inglés		la lengua española		las ciencias	
miércoles	el inglés		el dibujo	la educación física	libre	
jueves	el dibujo	la música	la lengua española	la historia	la educación física	
viernes	la música	las matemáticas	la geografía	las ciencias	la informática	

Ejercicio 2 **Responde a las preguntas.**
Reply to the questions.

Me gusta el dibujo. Es divertido.
¿Y a tí? _____

Me gustan las matemáticas. Son interesantes.
¿Y a ti?
_____

Me gusta la música. Es genial.
¿Y a ti?
_____

No me gusta la educación física. Es aburrida.
¿Y a ti?
_____

No me gusta el inglés. Es bastante difícil.
¿Y a ti?
_____

¡Es Español! © Kathy Williams and Beatriz Rubio

¡A comer!

Learning objectives

Pupils will be able to:

* Talk about food for a picnic
* Say 'I would like ...', 'please' and 'thank you'.
* Use numbers up to 100

Resources needed

* Sheets 14a, 14b, 14c, 14d, 14e; CD Track 20.
* Real food items (bread, butter, ham, cheese, crisps, etc); tablecloths; notepads for 'waiters'; sticky labels; variety of goods 'for sale'.

Activities

* Talk about what foods you might take on a picnic. Using the flashcards on sheet 14a (or the real thing) introduce the phrase '¿Quieres ...?'. Pupils choose from what is on offer. Pupils reply using 'sí/no'. The CD introduces 'quiero ...' at the same time. Pupils could use this phrase to ask for items. If you are using real food, you could have a picnic (un picnic) at this stage.

* Sheet 14b reinforces choices – pupils draw chosen foods (you could limit it to five or six) then explain what they would like for a picnic to a partner/to the group. (Revise 'Me gusta/me gustan ...' Units 10 and 13).

* Sheet 14a can also be used to play a game. Cut up two sheets to make 18 cards. Pupils play in groups of six, having three cards each to start. The aim is to collect all the food from the other players. Player 1 starts by asking anyone else for a card by saying, eg 'Quiero pan,' to collect a food item he/she does not have; or has only one card of the two.

Vocabulario – Key words

quiero	I would like
¿quieres ...?	do you want ...?
pan (m)	bread
mantequilla (f)	butter
queso (m)	cheese
jamón (m)	ham
chocolate (m)	chocolate
Coca-Cola (f)	cola
patatas fritas (f)	crisps/chips
manzanas (f)	apples
un té	a tea
un café	a coffee
un agua mineral	a mineral water
un zumo de naranja	an orange juice
un zumo de fruta	a fruit juice
un perrito caliente	a hot dog
un bocadillo	a baguette
un sandwich	a sandwich
un croissant	a croissant
un sandwich (de jamón/ de queso)	a sandwich (with ham/ with cheese)
¿qué van a tomar?	what are you having?
aquí tiene(n)	here you are
gracias	thank you
por favor	please
son 50 euros	that comes to 50 euros
pasteles	cakes

If that person has the requested card he/she hands it over saying 'aquí tienes'. Player 1 continues until he/she makes a mistake by asking for a card that someone does not have. It is then that player's turn to say 'Quiero …' to another player. He may, of course, ask for the card that Player 1 has just acquired. This game tests memory as well as vocabulary!

✳ ✎ Listen to the food vocabulary on the CD. Use sheet 14c to help identify food/drink items ordered in the café. Fill in vocabulary. Highlight '¿Qué van a tomar?' and use of 'un té/una Coca-Cola', etc.

✳ Pupils could design their own café menus. You could talk about different Spanish eating places and the café culture of Spain. Dictionaries could be used to expand the dishes/drinks on offer.

✳ ✎ Build up a café dialogue using phrases already learned. Pupils can fill in the gaps on sheet 14d. Highlight prices in the menu, please and thank you.

✳ Using pupils' menus and tables laid out café-style, pupils role-play a café scene. You could record or video for the class or others. Encourage use of further conversation if possible particularly stating opinions about the food (Units 9, 10 and 13).

✳ ✎ Listen to and practise numbers up to 100. Sheet 14e helps to reinforce larger numbers.

Further activities

✳ Pupils could design a poster to advertise their café. They could use ICT facilities to print a poster/flier.

✳ Pupils could research Spanish regional dishes and products.

✳ Numbers practice can come from a guessing game based on 'Supermarket Sweep' (or other such TV programmes). Present pupils with a variety of goods in a wide price range. Stick a label on the base of each with a price in euros from 1–100. Look up the exchange rate in a newspaper or on teletext. Pupils guess (in teams) what the prices could be. The team with the closest amount wins a point, and the most correct/close answers wins the game.

¡Es Español! © *Kathy Williams and Beatriz Rubio*

Para un picnic

For a picnic (flashcards)

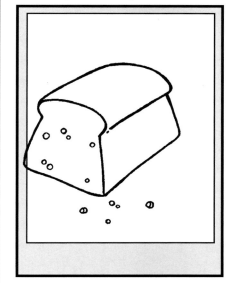

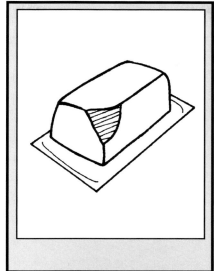

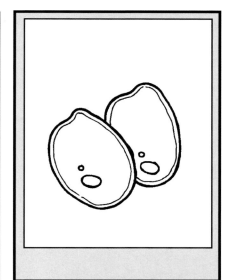

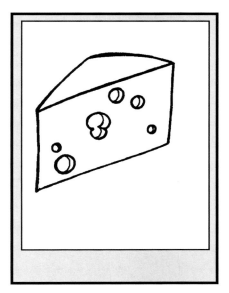

¿Quieres ir de picnic?

Do you want a picnic?

Elige lo que quieres para hacer un picnic. Dibújalos en el mantel.

Choose what you would like for a picnic. Draw them on the tablecloth.

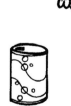

¡Es Español! © Kathy Williams and Beatriz Rubio

En el café

At the café

Quiero ...   **y ....**
I would like ...   *and ...*

 _____    _____

 _____    _____

 _____    _____

 _____   _____

 _____   _____

_____   _____

un té   una Coca-Cola

un zumo de naranja

un agua mineral

un café con leche

un zumo de fruta

un croissant

un bocadillo de queso

un sandwich de jamón

patatas fritas   un perrito caliente

un bocadillo de jamón

¿Qué van a tomar?

What are you having?

Mira el menú.

Look at the menu.

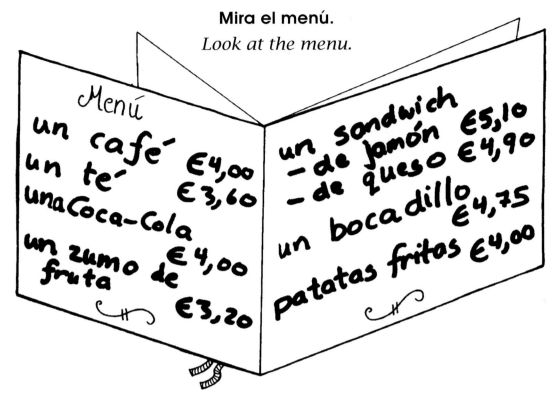

Menú

un café €4,00
un té €3,60
una Coca-Cola €4,00
un zumo de fruta €3,20

un sandwich
– de jamón €5,10
– de queso €4,90
un bocadillo €4,75
patatas fritas €4,00

Lee la conversación. Rellena los espacios:

Read the conversation. Fill in the spaces:

Pedro: ¿Quieres una Coca-Cola, Isabel?

Isabel: Sí, quiero una Coca-Cola.

Pedro: Quiero un _____

Isabel: Quiero un sandwich de _____

El camarero: Hola, ¿qué van a tomar?

Pedro: Quiero un _____ por favor.

Isabel: Para mí, un sandwich de _____ , patatas fritas y
una Coca-Cola, por favor.

El camarero: Aquí tienen, una _____ , un _____ , un
sandwich de _____ y _____.
Son _____ euros.

Pierre: Aquí tiene. Gracias.

¡Es Español! © **Kathy Williams and Beatriz Rubio**

Los números 20–100+

Numbers 20-100+

20 – veinte
30 – treinta
40 – cuarenta
50 – cincuenta
60 – sesenta
70 – setenta
80 – ochenta
90 – noventa
100 – cien

21 – veintiuno	35 – treinta y cinco
31 – treinta y uno	47 – cuarenta y siete
41 – cuarenta y uno	53 – cincuenta y tres
51 – cincuenta y uno	64 – sesenta y cuatro
61 – sesenta y uno	79 – setenta y nueve
71 – setenta y uno	86 – ochenta y seis
81 – ochenta y uno	98 – noventa y ocho
91 – noventa y uno	

101 – ciento uno	200 – doscientos
102 – ciento dos	201 – doscientos uno
150 – ciento cincuenta	250 – doscientos cincuenta

¿Sabes escribir estos números?

Can you write these numbers?

36 – treinta ____ _____

46 – cuarenta ___ _____

57 – cincuenta ___ _____

63 – _____ ___ _____

72 – _____ ___ _____

89 – _____ ___ _____

94 – _____ ___ _____

108 – _____ _____

Hago deporte

Learning objectives

Pupils will be able to:

* Talk about parts of the body
* Name some common sports
* Express opinions about sports

Resources needed

* Sheets 15a, 15b, 15c, 15d, 15e; CD Tracks 21–22.
* Dice.

Activities

* Teach parts of the body by saying the name and touching the corresponding part of the body. Repeat a few times.

* Ask pupils to give examples of body parts that they remember from the teacher's expanations and actions.

* Sheet 15a is a vocabulary matching exercise for parts of the body. Pupils can listen to the CD to clarify choices. (The answers are given in the correct order, first for the left side, then the right.)

* In groups of three or four, give each pupil a person from sheet 15b, together with chopped up pieces of the same character. Each piece is numbered. Player 1 throws the dice and picks up one part of his person with that number on, stating the body part(s) pictured. The winner is the first player to complete his/her figure.

* Pupils react to the CD by touching the part of the body mentioned after 'Tócate …'. They could then practise the same commands and responses in pairs. 'Tócate' is the singular form of 'Tacaos' used in Unit 2 (in the plural form).

* Sheet 15c extends the exercise theme by introducing various sports. Pupils listen to the CD and identify which sport is being referred to. They write the corresponding letters in the gaps. You could ask them to give their responses to the group using the alphabet in Spanish.

Vocabulario – Key words

la cabeza	head
la pierna	leg
la boca	mouth
la mano	hand
el pie	foot
la rodilla	knee
el brazo	arm
la nariz	nose
el estómago	stomach
el pelo	hair
los ojos	eyes
las orejas	ears
el hombro	shoulder
hago	I do
juego	I play
juego al/a la + sport	I play …
hago + sport	I do …

¡Es Español! © *Kathy Williams and Beatriz Rubio*

✱ Remind pupils of 'Me gusta/n …', 'No me gusta/n …' (Unit 10). Introduce 'Hago …' and recall 'Juego …' (Unit 13).

✱ 🎧 Ask pupils the question '¿Qué deportes haces?' as modelled on CD and note replies from three or more other pupils , writing their names in the sport boxes at the bottom of sheet 15c. Pupils should use 'Hago/juego' to reply.

✱ Pupils could fill in the pie-chart on sheet 15d (gráfico) to show the popularity of different sports. You could talk about sports which are popular in Spain and about any Spanish sports stars or teams that pupils have seen or heard of.

✱ Pupils could use dictionaries to compile an extended list of sports in Spanish.

✱ Sheet 15e (CD Track 22): song 'A mi burro'. This song is about a donkey which has pains everywhere. Students could listen to the song and recognize the parts of the body. The song could also be sung. It can be as long as you like, just add different body parts for each verse.

Further activities

✱ To practise body parts, pupils draw a head and neck on the top third of a piece of paper. They fold the paper backwards so that only the neck is showing and pass the paper to someone else. The next person draws the body and the start of the legs, folding the paper back, handing it to someone else to draw the legs and feet. This is then passed to a fourth person who opens out the page to reveal a full body. They then name the resulting body parts to the group, pointing them out as they do so.

✱ Pupils could mime sporting actions to each other to identify the sport.

✱ Whisper game: pupils close their eyes and touch the part of their body that you or another pupil whispers to them. Players are out if they are touching the wrong part when they open their eyes.

✱ Mini 'tabla de ejercicios'. This game practises numbers as well as body parts. Compile together a list of 'ejercicios', eg 'Tocaos la nariz veinte veces' (touch your nose 20 times), 'Tocaos la oreja con el hombro doce veces' (touch your ear with your shoulder 12 times). Each exercise is then performed in pairs with the pupils counting out in Spanish as they do them.

El cuerpo humano

The human body

Rellena los huecos.

Fill in the blanks.

la c_____

las o_____

el p_____

los o_____

la n_____

la m_____

la b_____

el b_____

el h_____

el e_____

la p_____

la r_____

los p_____

la cabeza   las orejas   la nariz

los pies   el brazo   el estómago   la boca

la pierna   la rodilla   la mano   los ojos

el hombro   el pelo

¡Es Español!   © Kathy Williams and Beatriz Rubio

Las cartas

¡Es Español!

Hago gimnasia

I do gymnastics

¿Qué deportes haces?
What sports do you do?

👂 **Escucha y escribe la letra que corresponda con cada deporte:**
Listen and write the letters to match the names of the sports:

_____
D
_____
_____
_____
_____
_____

A fútbol

B rugby

C atletismo

D baloncesto

E gimnasia

F ciclismo

G natación

H tenis

¿Qué deportes haces? Una encuesta
What sports to you do? A survey

Hago	ciclismo	atletismo	natación	gimnasia
Juego	al fútbol	al rugby	al tenis	al baloncesto

Un gráfico circular de deportes

A sports pie-chart

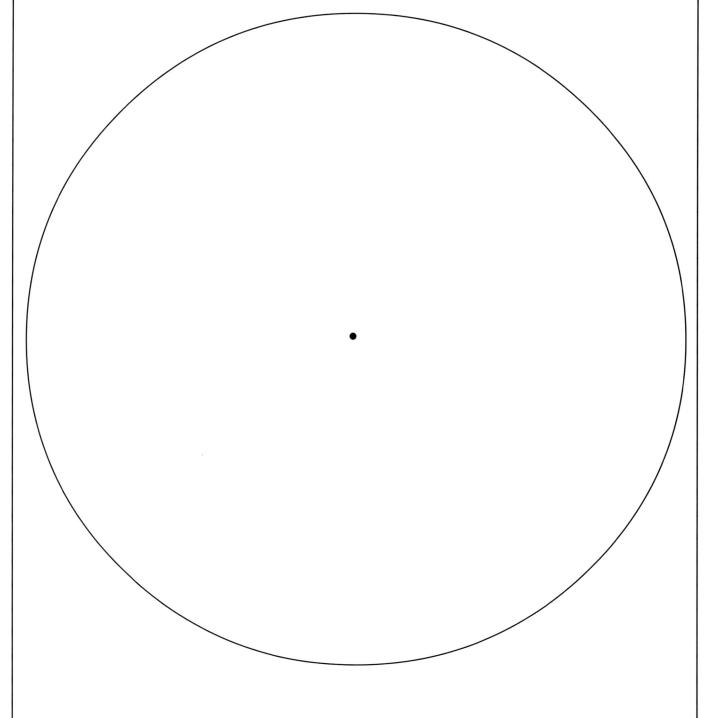

Éstos son los deportes que hacemos en mi clase.

Here are the sports that people do in my class.

¡Es Español!
www.brilliantpublications.co.uk

A mi burro

My donkey

Canta esta canción.
Sing this song.

A mi burro, a mi burro le duele la cabeza
y el médico le ha dado una gorrita gruesa
una gorrita gruesa, mi burro enfermo está,
mi burro enfermo está.

A mi burro a mi burro le duelen las orejas
y el médico le ha dado un jarro de cerveza
un jarro de cerveza, mi burro enfermo está,
mi burro enfermo está.

A mi burro, a mi burro le duele la garganta
y el médico le ha dado una bufanda blanca
una bufanda blanca, mi burro enfermo está,
mi burro enfermo está.

A mi burro, a mi burro le duele el corazón
y el médico la ha dado gotitas de limón
gotitas de limón, mi burro enfermo está
mi burro enfermo está.

A mi burro, a mi burro le duelen las rodillas
y el médico le ha dado un frasco con pastillas
un frasco con pastillas, mi burro enfermo está,
mi burro enfermo está.

¡Es Español!   © *Kathy Williams and Beatriz Rubio*

Unit 16 — La ropa

Learning objectives

Pupils will be able to:

✱ Name some common items of clothing
✱ Say what they wear for different occasions
✱ Describe their clothes

Resources needed

✱ Sheet 16a, 16b, 16c, 16d; CD Tracks 23–24.
✱ TV recordings of people; real clothing items; large bag; clothes catalogues/magazine pictures.

Activities

✱ ☞ Introduce the names of items of clothing. Pupils could either refer to sheet 16a (ideally enlarged) or to real items of clothing. The clothes are pictured on the sheet as if they are in a shop window (with the words removed).

✱ Use real items of clothing or point to an item on the sheet. Suggest to one class member that he/she can take it, eg '¿Para ti ... la falda?' Pupils could accept, or refuse and make another choice.

✱ Using a large bag containing clothes, reveal and name one item at a time. Replace them in the bag and ask pupils if they can remember what items were taken out of the bag and name the clothes in Spanish.

✱ Pupils match the words from the bottom of sheet 16a with the items pictured. They could cut out the labels and stick them on the picture.

✱ Pupils could colour in their clothes sheets then use the sheets as a class exercise to revise colours (from Units 9 and 10) as individuals say which colours they have chosen for their clothing.

✱ ☞ Extend discussion of adjectives to include 'grande' or 'pequeño' (from Unit 10), and 'largo' or 'corto'. Pupils could practise using the adjectives by talking about the items on sheet 16a to a partner.

Vocabulario – Key words

los pantalones	trousers
los vaqueros	jeans
la camiseta	T-shirt
los pantalones cortos	shorts
el sombrero	hat
la corbata	tie
la falda	skirt
el vestido	dress
la chaqueta	jacket
los calcetines	socks
los zapatos	shoes
las zapatillas de deporte	trainers
largo/a	long
corto/a	short
grande	big
pequeño	small
llevo	I wear, I am wearing
una fiesta	a party

✱ ♫ The agreement of adjectives is explained on the CD. To form the feminine adjective the 'o' of the masculine form is removed and replaced by an 'a'. Explain also that 'grande' is invariable; gender changes do not apply to it.

✱ Photocopy sheet 16b onto card and cut out the dominoes. Pupils play the game in threes or fours. Player 1 places a double domino on the table. Player 2 must add the opposite to one already down, so if a double noun is on the table, then an adjective should be placed next to one end of the domino. If a player cannot go, the turn passes on to the next player. If no-one can take a turn, the next player puts a new double domino card down and the game continues. The winner is the first player to get rid of all his/her dominoes or to have the least number of dominoes left when a maximum of two fresh starts have been made. The sequence of words along the chain should always be matching nouns and adjectives: this practises recognition of 'roja' as a feminine adjective that can only match with 'una falda', 'azul' as an adjective which can go with both 'una falda' and 'un vestido' and 'marrones' as a plural adjective that can only be matched with the plural noun 'unos zapatos'.

✱ Pupils could cut out catalogue pictures, and describe what they like about their choice of outfit, eg 'Me gusta la falda negra y la camiseta roja.' Highlight again gender of adjectives and the fact that, unlike English, adjectives go after the noun.

✱ ♫ 'Llevo …' is introduced. Pupils use cut-out pictures or do drawings to illustrate four different types of outfit. They describe to the group what they have chosen – the clothes could be used for fashion display. Sheet 16c provides a useful visual prompt.

✱ ♫ Sheet 16d (CD Track 24). La Tarara. Pupils listen to the song. What items of clothing are mentioned in the song? What colour are they?

Further activities

✱ Use a video recording of a TV show (any show where people are easily seen and clothes can be identified). Show the video with sound; afterwards ask the pupils to name the items of clothing that they saw people wearing.

✱ The above activity can be extended to describing the colour and size of clothing, and hair/eye colour (Unit 11). You could arrange for someone to come into the class briefly on some pretext – then afterwards ask pupils to say what he/she was wearing, what he/she looked like and so on.

✱ Pupils could play 'I Spy' in pairs with sheet 16a, revising letters of the alphabet.

✱ Pupils could plan their own 'fashion show'. They could video it and overlay a commentary describing the clothes in Spanish.

¡Es Español!   © *Kathy Williams and Beatriz Rubio*

La ropa

Clothes

los pantalones	los vaqueros	los pantalones cortos	el sombrero
la camiseta	los zapatos	los calcetines	las zapatillas de deporte
el vestido	la falda	la corbata	la chaqueta

Corta y pega los nombres de las ropas.

Cut out and stick the labels on the pictures of the clothes.

Dominos

roja	roja	una falda	una falda	azul	azul
unos zapatos	unos zapatos	marrones	marrones	un vestido	un vestido
roja	una falda	una falda	un vestido	marrones	unos zapatos
una falda	roja	unos zapatos	roja	azul	roja
roja	un vestido	roja	unos zapatos	marrones	un vestido
marrones	roja	un vestido	marrones	un falda	un vestido
marrones	azul	una falda	azul	un vestido	azul
unos zapatos	roja	unos zapatos	un vestido	azul	una falda
azul	una falda	azul	unos zapatos	un vestido	unos zapatos
unos zapatos	marrones	una falda	marrones	un vestido	marrones

¡Es Español!   © Kathy Williams and Beatriz Rubio

Llevo ...

I wear ...

A la escuela llevo ...

At school I wear ...

De vacaciones llevo ...

On holiday I wear ...

Para hacer deporte llevo ...

To do sport I wear ...

A una fiesta llevo ...

At a party I wear ...

¡Es Español!   95
www.brilliantpublications.co.uk

La Tarara

The Tarara

Canta esta canción.

Sing this song.

Tiene la Tarara un vestido blanco que solo se pone en el Jueves Santo.
La Tarara sí, La Tarara no, La Tarara madre que la bailo yo.

Tiene La Tarara unos pantalones que de arriba a abajo todo son botones.
La Tarara sí, La Tarara no, La Tarara madre que la bailo yo.

Tiene La Tarara un vestido verde lleno de volantes y de cascabeles.
La Tarara sí, La Tarara no, La Tarara madre que la bailo yo.

¡Es Español!   © *Kathy Williams and Beatriz Rubio*

En mi pueblo

Learning objectives

Pupils will be able to:

* Name common town places/ buildings
* Say where places are (left, right, here, there)
* Describe the location of their home town
* Use points of the compass

Resources needed

* Sheet 17a, 17b, 17c; CD Track 25.
* Town plans; tourist brochures; model buildings (childrens' wooden toys for example); names of buildings on large signs.

Activities

*) Listen to the description on the CD of Buenpueblo, an imaginary town. The words for various buildings are introduced.

* Use town plans and tourist brochures of different places, eg London, Madrid, Oxford. Alternatively, list of buildings in your home town. Pupils suggest Spanish names for landmarks or buildings. Go through resulting list as a group. Look for cognates (words with similar origins), eg 'banco – bank'.

* In pairs pupils could play buildings snap. Photocopy sheet 17a onto card and cut out the cards. Each player gets 12. They each put down a card at the same time. Pupils say the Spanish word when the pictures on the two piles match. The first to say the word collects the cards. The winner is the first player to collect all the cards.

* Sheet 17b reinforces some vocabulary. Pupils have to solve the anagrams to make building words. You could give them more words to muddle for friends to unravel.

*) Introduce the use of 'a la izquierda' and 'a la derecha' when giving directions.

Vocabulario – Key words

correos	post office
el banco	bank
la estación	station
la piscina	swimming pool
la comisaría	police station
el aparcamiento	car park
el monumento	monument
el museo	museum
el supermercado	supermarket
el hotel	hotel
la iglesia	church
la escuela	school
a la izquierda	on the left
a la derecha	on the right
aquí	here
allí	there
allá	over there
¿dónde está ...?	where is ...?
en el norte	in the north
... el sur	... south
... el este	... east
... el oeste	... west

✸   Using model buildings make a series of connecting streets, or draw a plan on the board. Pupils take turns to give a series of directions to get from one given point to another. The rest of the group follows the directions and says which building they have reached. The pupil who gave directions confirms or corrects.

✸   Blindfold one pupil and stand him/her in a set place, eg by the door. Another pupil, or group of pupils, gives him/her directions to arrive at a given spot. The blindfolded pupil must obey the instructions correctly. Further language such as 'sigue' (continue) and 'para' (stop) may be needed.

✸ 👂   'Aquí' (here) and 'allí' (there), and also 'allá' (over there), are introduced on the CD. Practise using them with the question '¿Dónde está …?'

✸   Stick large signs with building names from sheet 17a round the room. Ask, eg '¿Dónde está el banco?' Pupils point and say, eg 'Allí, a la izquierda'. Pupils walk around and 'meet' each other as if in the town square. They ask each other where places are and give an appropriate reply.

✸ 👂   Using sheet 17c, pupils listen to the description of where Madrid is in Spain (using points of the compass) and the buildings there.

✸ 👂   Listen to the description of Buenpueblo. Highlight the use of 'en el norte/el sur/el este/el oeste'. Pupils can try to identify which building is which on the 'Buenpueblo' plan and name them (sheet 17c).

✸   In groups, pupils could put together a list of places/facilities in their home town, and design a brochure to advertise it. This could be produced on computer or designed to be duplicated on a (colour) photocopier.

Further activities

✸   Pupils could test each other by miming actions connected with a particular building/place. Their partner must guess the place in Spanish.

✸   Pupils could draw town plans in groups of three or four using building words and suggesting '¿Aquí?'/'¿Allí?' when deciding where things should go, eg a hotel next to the main road or a church in the middle of the town.

✸   Pupils could research further information about Madrid or other major towns in Spain.

¡Es Español!   © *Kathy Williams and Beatriz Rubio*

Snap (flashcards)

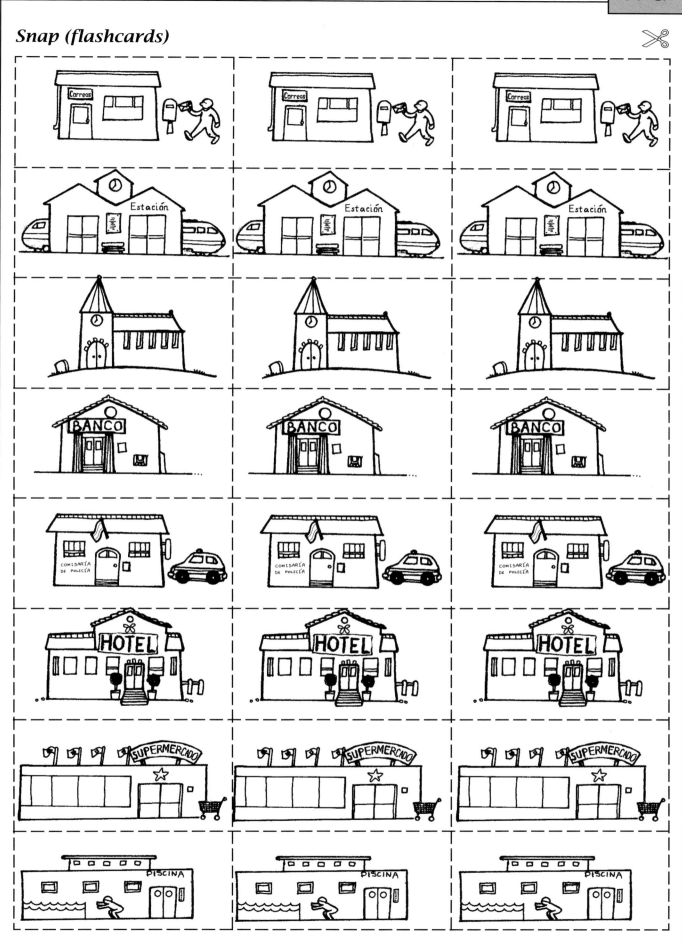

¡Es Español!

¿Qué es?

What is it?

The following are all anagrams. Fill in the blanks.

Aquí está:

Here is:

la igelasi = la _____

el merpersudoca = el _____

el osemu = el _____

la staóncie = la _____

el telho = el _____

la niscapi = la _____

¡Es Español!   © **Kathy Williams and Beatriz Rubio**

En la ciudad de Madrid

In Madrid

Madrid

el norte

el oeste   el este

el sur

•Buenpueblo

Escucha la descripión.

Listen to the description.

Un plano de Madrid

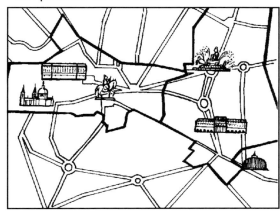

Un plano de Buenpueblo (una cuidad imaginaria)

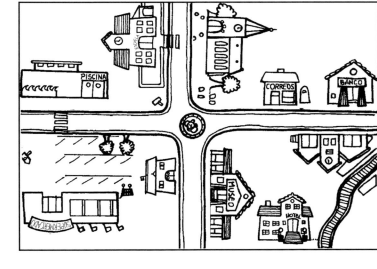

¿Dónde está?   ... el banco?
Where is?   ... correos?
                   ... el supermercado?

el aparacamiento   correos   el banco
la estación   el hotel   la iglesia   la escuela
el museo   la piscina   la comisaría
el supermercado

Ficha personal

Learning objectives

Pupils will be able to:

* Give a detailed description of themselves, drawing on material from several units
* Listen closely and understand longer descriptions of other people

Resources needed

* Sheet 18a.
* Pictures/photographs of famous people; video clips of well-known cartoon or programme characters.

Vocabulario – Key words

Personal descriptions from Units 1, 6, 8, 9, 11 and 17.

Interests and activities from Units 10, 7, 1 and 12.

Opinions from Units 14 and 16.

There are many additional links with other units.

Activities

* Display pictures/photographs of well-known people on a board. Describe a number of details about one of them using first person singular, eg 'Tengo el pelo gris', 'Tengo una hermana y dos hermanos' = picture of Prince Charles! Pupils have to guess which person is 'speaking'.

* Give pairs of pupils some time to note down a similar description of one of the other personalities. They then read their description for the class to guess.

* Pupils fill in sheet 18a without their names. The sheets are then redistributed and pupils either read them individually to work out who wrote it, or read the descriptions to the class who must put a name to the details.

* Pupils could also fill in sheet 18a, imagining that they are their favourite sports/ music star. Pictures from magazines and newspapers could be cut out to accompany these descriptions, making a good wall display.

* Pupils could present themselves on video and show this to a different year group at school.

* Using clips of well-known TV characters, encourage pupils to speak from visual prompts about the character as if that person were speaking, eg 'The Simpsons' – 'Me llamo Bart. Tengo una hermana. Tengo el pelo amarillo', etc.

Further activities

* Pupils could set up a 'Blind Date' show where three contestants describe themselves and the fourth must ask two or three questions about them using ideas from units in the course, eg '¿Tienes animales?' or '¿Te gusta el chocolate?' They then have to choose one of the three who have given the answers for a 'blind date'. The pupils could dress up and use this as a prompt to talk about their clothes, pretend to be from another country, or need everything to be spelled out for them. The language use is endless!

Una ficha personal

About myself

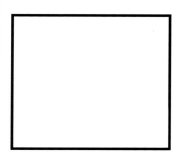

Me llamo_____.

Tengo _____ años.

Mi cumpleaños es el _____ .

Soy _____ .

Tengo _____ hermano(s). No tengo hermanos.

Tengo _____ hermana(s). No tengo hermanas.

Vivo en _____.

Vivo en _____.

Tengo el pelo _____.

Tengo los ojos _____.

Tengo un animal. Tengo _____.

Me gustan los _____.

Me gustan las _____.

En la escuela tengo _____ y _____.

Me gusta la historia y _____.

Me gusta la educación física.

Me gusta _____.

Llevo _____.

¡Hablo español!

Appendix

Grammar (gramática)

Unit 2/5

The indefinite article (a/an)

The word for 'a/an' can be either '**un**' or '**una**'. This depends on whether the noun following is masculine or feminine. All nouns in Spanish are either masculine or feminine. The table below shows examples:

	masculine noun			**feminine noun**	
un	niño	boy	**una**	niña	girl
	caballo	horse		regla	mouse
	lápiz	pen		silla	chair
	helado	ice-cream		escuela	school

Note: when counting 'one' is 'uno' not 'un'.

Unit 7

The definite article 'the' – singular

The word for 'the' is either '**el**' or '**la**' depending on whether the noun is masculine or feminine. The table below shows examples:

	masculine noun			**feminine noun**	
el	niño	boy	**la**	niña	girl
	caballo	horse		regla	mouse
	lápiz	pen		silla	chair
	helado	ice-cream		escuela	school

Unit 10

The definite article 'the' – plural

The word for 'the' when followed by a plural noun is '**los**' or '**las**' depending on whether the noun is masculine or feminine. For example:

Singular		Plural	
el niño	the boy	los niños	the boys
la niña	the girl	las niñas	the girls

¡Es Español! © Kathy Williams and Beatriz Rubio

Plural endings on nouns

Plural nouns in Spanish are formed by adding an -s to the singular of all nouns that finish with a vowel, and adding -es to those which finish with a consonant.

Singular		Plural	
el caballo	the horse	los caballos	the horses
la niña	a/one girl	las niñas	the girls
el ratón	a/one mouse	los ratones	the mice
el pez	a fish	los peces	the fishes

Note: If the consonant of the noun in singular is -z, it changes in the plural to 'c' and then -es is added.

Using the question '¿Te gusta/n ... ?' Do you like ... ?

In Spanish the use of ¿te gusta? or ¿te gustan? depends on whether the noun that follows is singular or plural. If it is singular the form adopted will be ¿te gusta ...?; on the other hand ¿te gustan ...? will be used if the noun is plural.

In Spanish the definite article must be included. The following examples show how the English corresponds to the Spanish.

Singular

¿Te gusta el queso?   Do you like cheese?
¿Te gusta el deporte?   Do you like sport?

Plural

¿Te gustan los perros?   Do you like dogs?
¿Te gustan las patatas? Do you like potatoes?

Demonstative pronouns

In Spanish 'this' in English takes two forms in the singular in Spanish according to the gender of the noun it refers to. If the noun is masculine the form is 'éste'; if the noun is feminine it is 'ésta'. There are some examples below:

Éste es mi padre.   This is my father.
Ésta es mi madre.   This is my mother.
Éste es mi hamster.   This is my hamster.
Ésta es mi bicicleta.   This is my bicycle.

Unit 11

The possesive

To say 'my' in Spanish, you choose either '**mi**' or '**mis**', depending on whether what belongs to you is singular or plural. Here are some examples:

my	singular noun	plural noun
mi	hermano	
mi	hermana	
mis		amigos (male friends)
mis		amigas (female friends)

Unit 16

Most adjectives in Spanish follow the noun that they are describing, for example:

una casa pequeña	a small house
un sombrero rojo	a red hat

Adjectives – agreement with nouns

When an adjective is used with a feminine noun the 'o' of the masculine adjective has to be removed and changed to an 'a'. Adjectives that end in a consonant or 'e', such as 'azul' or 'grande', are invariable and do not change when the gender of the noun changes. When an adjective is used with a plural noun an '-s' is added. There are some examples below:

	Masc. noun	Fem. noun	Pl. masc. noun	Pl. fem. noun
	un coche	una chaqueta	unos zapatos	unas camisas
red	rojo	roja	rojos	rojas
blue	azul	azul	azules	azules
big	grande	grande	grandes	grandes
small	pequeño	pequeña	pequeños	pequeñas
good	bueno	buena	buenos	buenas
beautiful	bonito	bonita	bonitos	bonitas
white	blanco	blanca	blancos	blancas
long	largo	larga	largos	largas

¡Es Español! © Kathy Williams and Beatriz Rubio

Background information

Unit 8 – Festivals celebrated in Spain.

La Nochebuena – Christmas Eve

Spanish people eat seafood, fish or lamb and 'turrón' (a kind of nougat) in a special late evening meal.

El día de Navidad – Christmas Day

Family day usually spent around the table. Another lavish meal similar to the night before is eaten and for pudding more 'turrón'.

Nochevieja

A celebration meal and 'cava' (Spanish champagne) leads into the New Year.

El día de Año Nuevo – New Year's Day

El día de los Reyes Magos – Twelfth Night

Children find presents in their bedrooms by their shoes, which they would have cleaned carefully the night before. Spanish people eat a 'Roscón de Reyes' a ring-shaped cake in which a little surprise is hidden.

El doce de octubre – 12th October

This national bank holiday commemorates the discovery of America in 1492 by Christopher Columbus.

Transcript of CD

Track 1

Nar: ¡Es Español!
Written by Kathy Williams and Beatriz Rubio. Copyright Brilliant Publications 2004.

Hola, hello, and welcome to '¡Es Español!'

In this recording you'll hear explanations to guide you through the units of '¡Es Español!'. All the key words are spoken on the recording, so you'll be able to listen to how they sound and practise repeating them. When learning new words it's better to listen to them first, before looking to see how they look when they are written down.

The recording also has exercises to test your understanding. You can pause the recording during these exercises to give yourself more time, and you can always replay any section.

Unit 1

Nar: **Unidad uno, Unit one. Hola.**
V 1: Hola. Hola.
*

V 1: ¿Cómo te llamas?
V 2: Me llamo Clara.
V 1: ¿Cómo te llamas?
*

V 2: ¿Cómo estás?
V 1: Bien, gracias. ¿Cómo estás?
V 2: Bien, gracias. ¿Cómo estás?
V 1: Bien, gracias.
*

V 1: Adiós. Adiós.
*

Nar: Here's the alphabet in Spanish. Notice how many of the letters have very similar names to the English names for them.
V 2: A B C D E F G H I J K L M N Ñ O P Q R S T U V W X Y Z.
*

Nar: What words are spelt out?
V 2: M-A-D-R-I-D
E-S-P-A-Ñ-A
H-O-L-A
E-S-P-A-Ñ-O-L

Nar: The answers are: Madrid, España, hola and español.

Track 2
Unit 2

Nar: **Unidad dos. Unit two. En clase.**
See if you can respond to these instructions correctly.
V 1: Levantaos. Muy bien.
Sentaos. Muy bien.
Escuchad. Muy bien.
Repetid 'Hola'. Muy bien.
Levantaos. Muy bien.
Mirad al profesor. Muy bien.
Sentaos. Muy bien.
*

Nar: If you need to speak to your teacher or ask something, it's polite to say:
V 2: Perdone. Perdone.
*

Nar: Sheet 2a. Here are some instructions used in the book.
V 1: Rellena; rellena los espacios.
V 2: Escribe; escribe los nombres.
V 1: Une; une los animales con sus nombres en español.
V 2: Escucha; escucha el CD.
V 1: Responde; responde a las preguntas.
V 2: Lee; lee el texto.
V 1: Completa; completa la lista.
V 2: Dibuja; dibuja una casa.
V 1: Encuentra; encuentra la palabra 'hola'.
*

Nar: Here are the names of some objects used in the classroom.
V 2: En clase.
V 1: Un lápiz, un bolígrafo, una cartera, un cuaderno, un sacapuntas, una regla, una goma, un estuche.
Nar: To say 'It is a pencil' or 'This is a pen' and so on, you say:
V 2: Es un lápiz. Es un bolígrafo. ¿Es un bolígrafo?
V 1: Sí. Sí.
V 2: ¿Es una regla?
V 1: No. No.
*

Nar: If you need to say that you do not have something:
V 1: Perdone, no tengo bolígrafo. No tengo bolígrafo.
*

¡Es Español! © Kathy Williams and Beatriz Rubio

Nar: Here's how to ask what something's called in Spanish:
V 2: ¿Cómo se dice en español? ¿Cómo se dice en español?

Track 3
Unit 3
Nar: **Unidad tres. Unit three. La semana.**
Here are the days of the week.
V 1: Los días de la semana: lunes, martes, miércoles, jueves, viernes, sábado, domingo.

✳

Nar: What day is it today?
V 1: ¿Qué día es hoy?
Nar: What are each of the following days?
V 2: Martes. Tuesday.
Viernes. Sí, Friday.
Lunes. Sí, es Monday.
Domingo. Sunday.
Miércoles. Muy bien, Wednesday.
Jueves. Thursday.
Sábado. Sí, Saturday.

Track 4
Unit 4
Nar: **Unidad cuatro. Unit four. Las estaciones y el tiempo.**
Sheet 4a. Here are some weather expressions.
V 1: Llueve.
V 2: Nieva.
V 1: Hace bueno.
V 2: Hace malo.
V 1: Hace viento; hace frío.
V 2: Hace sol; hace calor.

✳

V 1: ¿Qué tiempo hace hoy? ¿Hace bueno? ¿Llueve? ¿Qué tiempo hace hoy?

✳

V 2: ¿Qué tiempo hace ... en otoño?
Nar: Try to answer.
V 1: En otoño hace viento y llueve.
V 2: ¿Qué tiempo hace en invierno? ¿En invierno ...?
V 1: En invierno nieva y hace frío.
V 2: ¿Qué tiempo hace en primavera? ¿En primavera ...?
V1: En primavera hace bueno.
V 2: ¿Qué tiempo hace en verano? ¿En verano ...?
V 1: En verano hace sol y hace calor.

✳

Nar: Sheet 4d.
V 2: Escucha y escribe el número que corresponda.
Nar: Listen and write in a number next to each picture.
Number 1.
V 1: En verano hace calor y hace sol.
Nar: Number 2.
V 2: En invierno nieva.
Nar: Number 3.
V 1: En otoño hace viento.
Nar: Number 4.
V 2: En otoño llueve.
Nar: Number 5.
V 1: En primavera hace bueno.
Nar: Number 6.
V 2: En invierno hace malo ... y llueve.
✳

Track 5
Nar: Sheet 4e. Listen to the song '¡Qué llueva, qué llueva!'

Track 6
Unit 5
Nar: **Unidad cinco. Unit five. Los números del cero al veinte.**
Numbers from zero to twenty.
V 1: Los números del cero al diez: cero, uno, dos, tres, cuatro, cinco, seis, siete, ocho, nueve, diez.

✳

Nar: To ask someone to give you something you say:
V 2: Dame. Dame tres gomas, por favor.
✳

V 1: Los números del once al quince: once, doce, trece, catorce, quince.

✳

V 1: Los números del cero al veinte: cero, uno, dos, tres, cuatro, cinco, seis, siete, ocho, nueve, diez, once, doce, trece, catorce, quince, dieciséis, diecisiete, dieciocho, diecinueve, veinte.

✳

Track 7
Nar: Sheet 5d. Here's a song about elephants. It has the numbers up to nine: 'Un elefante'. Can you fill in the missing numbers on the sheet?

Track 8

Unit 6

Nar: **Unidad seis. Unit six. Me presento.**
Sheet 6a.

V 2: Escucha los nombres de las personas y las ciudades donde viven.

Nar: Match the people to the towns when you hear where they live.
Número 1.

V 1: Me llamo James. Vivo en Londres.

Nar: Número 2.

V 2: Me llamo Lucía. Vivo en Málaga.

Nar: Número 3.

V 1: Me llamo Miguel. Vivo en Sevilla.

Nar: Número 4.

V 2: Me llamo Clara. Vivo en Valencia.

Nar: Número 5.

V 1: Me llamo Pedro. Vivo en Santander.

Nar: Número 6.

V 2: Me llamo María. Vivo en Barcelona.

Nar: Número 7.

V 1: Me llamo Marcos. Vivo en Madrid.

Nar: Número 8.

V 2. Me llamo Elena. Vivo en La Coruña.

Nar: You can play this part of the recording again to fill in the numbers on Sheet 6b.

✱

Nar: Here's how to say where you live, and how to ask someone else where they live:

V 1: ¿Dónde vives?

V 2: Vivo en Londres. ¿Dónde vives?

V 1: Vivo en Madrid.

✱

V 2: ¿Cuál es tu dirección?

V 1: Mi dirección es calle de La Iglesia, 20. ¿Cuál es tu dirección?

V 2: Mi dirección es 15 Church Road.

Track 9

Unit 7

Nar: **Unidad siete. Unit seven. En casa.**
Sheet 7a. En casa. Rooms in the house.

V 1: La cocina.

V 2: El dormitorio.

V 1: El comedor.

V 2: El cuarto de baño.

V 1: El sótano.

V 2: El salón.

V 1: El ático.

V 2: El vestíbulo.

V 1: El garaje.

✱

Nar: Here's a description of somebody's house:

V 1: Ésta es una descripción de mi casa. En mi casa hay una cocina, un comedor y un salón. Hay un cuarto de baño y tres dormitorios.

✱

Nar: Where is Pedro? Listen and fill in the gaps on Sheet 7b.

V 2: ¿Dónde está Pedro?

V 1: En el dormitorio.

V 2: ¿Dónde está María?
¿Dónde está mamá?

V 1: ¿Dónde está papá?
¿Dónde está Luis?

V 2: ¿Dónde está el perro?
¿Dónde está el gato?

V 1: ¿Dónde está la araña?
¿Dónde está el ratón?

✱

Nar: Sheet 7c. Unos muebles. Some furniture.

V 1: Una cama, una silla, una mesa, un armario, una alfombra.

Track 10

Unit 8

Nar: **Unidad ocho. Unit eight. ¿Cuándo es tu cumpleaños?**
Here are the months in Spanish.

V 1: Los meses en español: enero, febrero, marzo, abril, mayo, junio, julio, agosto, septiembre, octubre, noviembre, diciembre.

✱

Nar: This is how to ask someone when their birthday is:

V 2: ¿Cuándo es tu cumpleaños? ¿Cuándo es tu cumpleaños?

V 1: Mi cumpleaños ... es en marzo. ¿Cuándo es tu cumpleaños?

V 2: Es en julio.

✱

Nar: To say when your birthday is, you need to know numbers up to 31. You already know numbers up to 20. Here are the numbers from 21 to 31.

V 1: Veintiuno, veintidós, veintitrés, veinticuatro, veinticinco, veintiséis, veintisiete, veintiocho, veintinueve, treinta, treinta y uno.

V 2: Mi cumpleaños es el diecisiete de febrero.

¡Es Español! © Kathy Williams and Beatriz Rubio

V 1: Mi cumpleaños es el veintiocho de
noviembre.

*

V1: Es mi cumpleaños.
V 2: ¡Feliz cumpleaños!

*

Track 11
Nar: Sheet 8b. This is how to sing Happy
Birthday in Spanish: '¡Cumpleaños feliz!'

*

Track 12
Nar: Sheet 8d. It's Christmas!
V 1: ¡Es Navidad!
Nar: Here are some Christmas words.
V 2: Un reno, un árbol de Navidad, un
muñeco de nieve, una estrella, Papá
Noel, un regalo.

Track 13
Unit 9
Nar: **Unidad nueve. Unit nine. Los países del
mundo.**
Sheet 9a. See if you can identify which
country in Europe each person comes
from. Carmen would say:
V 2: Me llamo Carmen. Vivo en España.
Nar: Dieter would say:
V 1: Me llamo Dieter. Vivo en Alemania.
Nar: Claudette would say:
V 2: Me llamo Claudette. Vivo en Francia.
Nar: Emilio would say:
V 1: Me llamo Emilio. Vivo en Italia.
Nar: Jane would say:
V 2: Me llamo Jane. Vivo en Inglaterra.
Nar: Gordon would say:
V 1: Me llamo Gordon. Vivo en Escocia.
Nar: Bernardette would say:
V 2: Me llamo Bernardette. Vivo en Irlanda.
Nar: David would say:
V 1: Me llamo David. Vivo en el País de
Gales.

Nar: The answers are:
V 2: España. Spain.
V 1: Alemania. Germany.
V 2: Francia. France.
V 1: Italia. Italy.
V 2: Inglaterra. England.
V 1: Escocia. Scotland.
V2: Irlanda. Ireland.
V 1: País de Gales. Wales.

*

Nar: Nationalities. Look at sheet 9a and
decide who each of these phrases refers
to:
V 1: Vive en Italia. Es italiano.
V 2: Vive en Francia. Es francesa.
V 1: Vive en Escocia. Es escocés.
V 2: Vive en Inglaterra. Es inglesa.
V 1: Vive en Irlanda. Es irlandesa.
V 2: Vive en Alemania. Es alemán.
V 1: Vive en España. Es española.
V 2: Vive en el País de Gales. Es galés.

Nar: Here are the answers:
V 1: Es italiano … Emilio.
Es francesa … Claudette.
Es escocés … Gordon.
Es inglesa … Jane.
Es irlandesa … Bernadette.
Es alemán … Dieter.
Es española … Carmen.
Es galés … David.

*

Nar: Using nationality words. Listen to the
nationalities of Claudette, Jane,
Bernadette and Carmen:
V 2: Francesa, inglesa, irlandesa, española.
Nar: In spelling as well as pronunciation there
is an 'a' at the end of the nationality
word when it applies to a female. To say
'I'm French', 'I'm English', 'I'm Irish' and
'I'm Spanish' if you are a boy, you say:
V 1: Soy francés, soy inglés, soy irlandés, soy
español.
Nar: Note that masculine nationalities that
finish in '–es' take an accent that
disappears in the feminine. So, if you are
a girl you say:
V 2: Soy francesa, soy inglesa, soy irlandesa,
soy española.

*

Nar: Sheet 9b. What colour is the Spanish
flag?
V 2: ¿De qué color es la bandera española?
V 1: La bandera española es roja, amarilla y
roja. Roja, amarilla y roja.
V 2: ¿Y la bandera italiana?
V 1: Verde, blanca y roja. Verde, blanca y
roja.
V 2: ¿Y la bandera alemana?
V 1: Negra, roja y amarilla. Negra, roja y
amarilla.

*

Nar: Some more colours:
V 2: Violeta, naranja, rosa. Violeta, naranja, rosa.
Nar: Use sheet 9c to help you to remember the colour words.

Track 14
Unit 10
Nar: **Unidad diez. Unit ten. ¿Te gustan los animales?**
Sheet 10a.
V 2: Un gato, un perro, un caballo, un pájaro, un conejo, un conejo de Indias, un pez, un ratón, una araña.

✳

Nar: This is how to ask someone if they like something:
V 2: ¿Te gustan los animales? ¿Te gustan los animales?
V 1: No, no me gustan los animales.
✳

Nar: To ask someone if they have a pet, you say:
V 2: ¿Tienes animales? ¿Tienes animales?
V 1: Sí, tengo un perro.
✳

Nar: Sheet 10d. Listen and decide which animal is being described.
V 1: ¿Qué animal es? Escucha las descripciones.
Nar: Número 1.
V 2: Es pequeño y naranja.
Nar: Número 2.
V 2: Es grande y gris.
Nar: Número 3.
V 2: Es blanco y negro. Es lindo.
Nar: Número 4.
V 2: Es pequeña y negra.
Nar: Número 5.
V 2: Es pequeño, azul y verde.
Nar: Número 6.
V 2: Es pequeño y blanco.
✳

Track 15
Nar: Sheet 10e. This song is about a very small mouse that was found under a button. 'Under a button'. 'Debajo de un botón'.

Track 16
Unit 11
Nar: **Unidad once. Unit eleven. Mi familia.**
V 1: Ésta es mi familia.
Éste es mi padre, mi padre.
Ésta es mi madre, mi madre.

✳

Nar: Can you remember how people introduce themselves?
V 1: Me llamo Roberto.
V 2: Me llamo Susana.
✳

Nar: This is how to ask if someone has brothers or sisters.
V 2: ¿Tienes hermanos? ¿Tienes hermanos?
V 1: Sí, tengo un hermano y una hermana. ¿Tienes hermanos?
V 2: No, no tengo.
✳

Nar: This is how to ask who someone is.
V 2: ¿Quién es?
V 1: Es mi padre, Felipe.
V 2: ¿Quién es?
V 1: Es mi hermana, Isabel.
✳

Nar: Sheet 11d. How to describe the colour of your hair and eyes.
V 1: Tengo los ojos marrones.
V 2 ¿Marrones?
V 1: Tengo los ojos azules.
V 2: ¿Azules?
V 1: Tengo los ojos verdes.
V 2: ¿Verdes?
V 1: Tengo los ojos negros.
V 2: ¿Negros?

V 2: Tengo el pelo moreno.
V1: ¿Moreno?
V 2: Tengo el pelo rojo.
V 1: ¿Rojo?
V 2: Tengo el pelo rubio.
V 1: ¿Rubio?
V 2: Tengo el pelo negro.
V 1: ¿Negro?
✳

Track 17
Nar: Sheet 11e. Here's a well-known Spanish song about families and names. The father was called José. 'José se llamaba el padre'.

¡Es Español! © Kathy Williams and Beatriz Rubio

Track 18
Unit 12

Nar: **Unidad doce. Unit twelve. De vacaciones.**
   To ask where someone is going, we say:
V 2: ¿Dónde vas? ¿Dónde vas?
V 1: Voy a la playa.
   Voy al campo.
   Voy a la montaña.

✳

Nar: If you're going to the mountain or the beach you say:
V 2: Voy a la montaña, voy a la playa.
Nar: However, if you're going to the countryside you say:
V 2: Voy al campo, voy al campo.

✳

Nar: Sheet 12b. Saying where you are going. You've already heard how to say to the beach, to the countryside, to the mountains:
V 1: A la playa, al campo, a la montaña.
Nar: When you want to say that you are going to a town we use the same expression 'voy a ...'. Listen to these phrases.
V 2: Voy a Madrid. Voy a Londres.

✳

Nar: You should also use 'voy a ...' to say that you are going to a country:
V 1: Voy a España. Voy a Inglaterra.

✳

Nar: Sheet 12c. Medios de transporte. Here are some forms of transport. This is what they're called in Spanish.
V 1: Un coche, un avión, una bicicleta, un autobús, un tren, un barco, un caballo, un pie.

✳

Nar: This is how you ask where someone is going.
V 1: ¿Dónde vas?
V 2: Voy a Madrid ... en avión. ¿Dónde vas?
V 1: Voy a Escocia ... en tren.

Track 19
Unit 13

Nar: **Unidad trece. Unit thirteen. Mi día.**
   Can you remember these weather expressions? See if you can say them in Spanish before the answer is given.
Nar: It's sunny.
V 1: Hace sol.
Nar: It's windy.
V 1: Hace viento.
Nar: It's fine.
V 1: Hace bueno.
Nar: It's not a nice day.
V 1: Hace malo.
Nar: It's hot.
V 1: Hace calor.
Nar: It's raining.
V 1: Llueve.
Nar: It's snowing.
V 1: Nieva.

✳

Nar: Sheet 13a. Look at the pictures. Choose which activity you think best fits the weather.
V 2: Cuando hace bueno ...
V 1: Cuando hace malo ...
V 2: Cuando nieva ...
V 1: Cuando hace sol ...
V 2: Cuando llueve ...

Nar: Have you worked out what 'cuando' means? 'Cuando' means 'when'.
V 1: Cuando hace bueno ... juego en el parque.
Nar: When it is fine ... I play in the park.

✳

Nar: Sheet 13b. Here are some activity phrases. Look at the sheet to work out what they mean.
V 1: Cuando hace sol ... juego en el jardín, juego en el jardín.
V 2: Cuando hace malo ... me quedo en casa, me quedo en casa.
V 1: Cuando llueve ... veo la televisión, veo la televisión.
Nar: See if you can make up some sentences yourself starting with: 'When it's sunny', 'when it is snowing' or 'when it's cold'.
V 1: Cuando hace sol ... juego en el parque.
V 2: Cuando nieva ... juego en el jardín.
V 1: Cuando hace frío ... me quedo en casa y veo la televisión.

✳

Nar: Sheet 13c. Listen to some of the things a child does in a day and put the pictures in the correct order.
V 1: Escucha y coloca los dibujos en orden.
V 2: Como el desayuno.
Llego a la escuela.
Escucho al profesor.
Trabajo en clase.
Vuelvo a casa.
Hablo con mis compañeros.

∗

Nar: To say the time, you start with 'Es la …' only if it is one o'clock. Use 'Son las …' the rest of the time.
V 1: Son las siete.
V 2: Son las nueve.
V 1: Es la una.
V 2: Son las dos.
V 1: Son las tres.
V 2: Son las cuatro.
V 1: Es la una.
¿Qué hora es? ¿Qué hora es?
V 2: Son las once.

∗

Nar: Here are some school subjects.
V 1: Éstas son algunas asignaturas en la escuela.
V 2: Las matemáticas, las ciencias, la educación física, la lengua española, el dibujo, el inglés, la historia, la geografía, la música, la informática.

∗

Nar: Sheet 13e. ¿Qué día es? Listen and decide which days on Javier's timetable are being described:
V 1: A las nueve tengo inglés, a las once tengo lengua española, y a las dos tengo ciencias.
V 2: Es martes.
V 1: A las nueve, tengo música y a las diez tengo matemáticas. A las dos tengo informática.
V 2: Es viernes.
V 1: A las once tengo dibujo y a las doce tengo educación físcia.
V 2: Es miércoles.

∗

Nar: You could use the following words to describe school subjects. Can you guess what they mean?
V 1: Divertido, interesante, genial, aburrido, bastante difícil.

Track 20
Unit 14
Nar: **Unidad catorce. Unit fourteen. A comer.** Sheet 14a. What do you want for a picnic?
V 1: ¿Quieres pan? ¿Sí? ¿No?
¿Quieres mantequilla? ¿Jamón?
¿Queso? ¿Chocolate? ¿Coca-Cola?
¿Quieres patatas fritas? ¿Quieres manzanas? ¿Quieres pasteles?
V 2: ¡Mmm! ¡Sí! Quiero pan, jamón y patatas fritas.

∗

Nar: Sheet 14c. En el café. Here are some foods you could buy at the café.
V 2: Una Coca-Cola, un té, un café con leche, un agua mineral, un zumo de fruta, un zumo de naranja.
V 1: Un perrito caliente, un bocadillo de queso, un sandwich de jamón, patatas fritas, un croissant, un bocadillo de jamón.

∗

Nar: Sheet 14d. Choosing at the café.
V 1: ¿Qué van a tomar?
V 2: Ah sí, quiero una Coca-Cola, un café con leche y un sandwich de jamón, por favor.
V 1: ¡Aquí tienen!
V 2: Gracias.
Nar: ¿Qué van a tomar? What are you having? Remember to say please 'por favor' and thank you 'gracias'.

∗

Nar: When you're buying food and drink, you need to be able to understand and say numbers beyond thirty. You have already heard the numbers up to 31. Here are some larger numbers that might be helpful to understand prices:
V 1: Cuarenta, cincuenta, sesenta.
Nar: Forty, fifty, sixty.
V 1: Cuarenta y cuatro, cincuenta y seis, sesenta y nueve.
Nar: Forty-four, fifty-six, sixty-nine.
V 1: Setenta, setenta y dos, setenta y siete.
Nar: Seventy, seventy-two, seventy-seven.
V 1: Ochenta, ochenta y cinco, noventa.
Nar: Eighty, eighty-five, ninety.
V 1: Noventa y nueve.
Nar: Ninety-nine.

¡Es Español!

V 1:   Cien, ciento cincuenta, doscientos.
Nar: One hundred, one hundred and fifty, two hundred.

Track 21
Unit 15
Nar: **Unidad quince: Unit fifteen. Hago deporte.**
       Sheet 15a. Here are the names for parts of the body.
V 1:   El cuerpo humano.
V 2:   El pelo, los ojos, la nariz, la boca, el hombro, la pierna.
V 1:   La cabeza, las orejas, la mano, el brazo, el estómago, la rodilla, los pies.

*

Nar: Tócate – touch the correct part of your body.
 1:    Tócate la cabeza.
V 2:   Tócate las orejas.
V 1:   Tócate el estómago.
V 2:   Tócate la pierna.
V 1:   Tócate los pies.
V 2:   Tócate el hombro.
V 1:   Tócate la nariz
V 2:   Tócate la rodilla.
V 1:   Tócate el pelo.

*

Nar: Sheet 15c. What are these sports?
V 2:   Es atletismo.
V 1:   Es natación.
V 2:   Es baloncesto.
V 1:   Es tenis.
V 2:   Es ciclismo.
V 1:   Es fútbol.
V 2:   Es rugby.
V 1:   Es gimnasia.

*

Nar: If you want to ask someone what sports they do:
V 1:   ¿Qué deportes haces? ¿Qué deportes haces?
V 2:   Hago ciclismo y … juego al tenis.

*

Track 22
Nar: 'A mi burro'. Listen to this song about a donkey that has aches and pains everywhere. How many parts of the body can you recognize?

Track 23
Unit 16
Nar: **Unidad dieciséis. Unit sixteen. La ropa.**
       Here are some clothes.
V 1:   Los pantalones, los vaqueros, los pantalones cortos, el sombrero.
V 2:   La camiseta, los zapatos, los calcetines, las zapatillas de deporte.
V 1:   El vestido, la falda, la corbata, la chaqueta.

*

Nar: To describe our clothes we need to use some adjectives like big:
V 1:   Grande.
Nar: Small.
V 2:   Pequeño.
Nar: Long.
V 1:   Largo.
Nar: And short.
V 2:   Corto.
*

Nar: Sheet 16a. Which words would you use to describe the hat, the dress and the skirt?
V 1:   El sombrero es pequeño, pequeño.
V 2:   El vestido es largo, largo.
Nar: What about the skirt?
V 1:   La falda es corta, corta.
Nar: Notice how when the item of clothing is feminine, as in the last example 'la falda', the 'o' of the masculine adjective 'corto' is removed and replaced by an 'a' 'corta'. Listen to how it works.
V 2:   Un sombrero pequeño.
       Una falda pequeña.
       Un vestido largo.
       Una camiseta larga.
Nar: Note how grande is invariable. That means that it doesn't change when it is used with a masculine or a feminine noun.
V 1:   Un vestido grande.
       Una camiseta grande.
Nar: If the clothing described is in plural, for example, a pair of trousers 'los pantalones' we add and 's' to the adjective.
V 1:   Grandes, los pantalones grandes.
V 2:   Pequeños, los pantalones pequeños.
Nar: If the items of clothing are feminine, we also add an 's' to the singular.

V 1: las chaquetas grandes.
V 2: las chaquetas pequeñas.
∗

Nar: Sheet 16c. What do you wear for different occasions and activities?
V 1: A la escuela llevo ...
V 2: De vacaciones llevo ...
V 1: Para hacer deporte llevo ...
V 2: A una fiesta llevo ...
∗

Track 24
Nar: Sheet 16d. Listen to the song 'La Tarara'. What items of clothing are mentioned? What colour are they?

Track 25
Unit 17
Nar: **Unidad diecisiete. Unit seventeen. En mi pueblo.**
Listen to the description of an imaginary town called Buenpueblo.
V 1: En Buenpueblo hay muchos edificios. Hay una estación, una piscina, correos, y un banco en la calle principal. En el centro del pueblo está la comisaría, el museo y el monumento. También hay un supermercado, un aparcamiento, un hotel y la iglesia.

∗

Nar: To give directions we use:
V 1: A la izquierda, a la izquierda.
V 2: A la derecha, a la derecha.
V 1: La piscina está a la izquierda.
V 2: El museo está a la derecha.
∗

Nar: Do you remember how to ask where someone or something is?

V 1: ¿Dónde está ...? ¿Dónde está ...? ¿Dónde está el banco? ¿Dónde está el banco, por favor?
V 2: El banco está aquí, a la izquierda.
V 1: ¿Dónde está correos?
V 2: Correos está allí, a la derecha.
V 1: ¿Dónde está la iglesia?
V 2: La iglesia está allá.
∗

Nar: Sheet 17c. Here's a description of Madrid. Can you hear some names and landmarks?
V 2: Una descripción de Madrid. Madrid es la capital de España. Madrid está en el centro de España. En la ciudad hay museos y monumentos e iglesias como La Almudena. Hay grandes hoteles come el Palace y grandes estaciones como la Estación de Atocha.
∗

V 1: ¿Y Buenpueblo?
Nar: And what about our town, Buenpueblo.
V 1: Buenpueblo está en el sur de España. En Buenpueblo hay un monumento en el centro del pueblo. A la izquierda, están la piscina, la comisaría y la escuela. También el supermercado y el aparcamiento. A la derecha están la iglesia, el museo, el hotel, correos, el banco y la estación.

∗

Nar: You've now reached the end of the recording. Thank you for listening.
V 1: ¡Adiós!
V 2: ¡Adiós!

¡Es Español!   © Kathy Williams and Beatriz Rubio

English translations of songs

¡Qué llueva, qué llueva! page 23
Let's hope it rains, it rains!

Let's hope it rains, it rains!
The virgin of the cave
The birds sing
The clouds rise
Yes, no, let's hope it pours down
Let's hope it pours down with sugar and lemon!

Un elefante page 29
One elephant

One elephant was rocking/swinging on a
   cobweb,
As he saw it resisted he called another elephant.

Two elephants, etc.

¡Cumpleaños feliz! page 42
Happy Birthday!

Happy birthday to you
Happy birthday to you
We all wish you
Happy birthday

Happy birthday
We all wish you
And that for many years
You can celebrate your birthday.

Cumplir: to be, to reach the age of, to turn, as in
'to turn twenty' – 'cumplir veinte años'.

Debajo un botón page 56
Under a button

Under one of Mr Martin's buttons, there was a tiny
   mouse
How tiny was the mouse that Mr Martin found
   under a button.

Mr Martin is so playful that he put the mouse in a
   sock.
In a sock lives that mouse, Mr Martin put him there
   because he is playful.

José se llamaba el padre page 63
The father was called José

José was called the father
Josefa his wife
And they had a young son called …

A mi burro page 90
My donkey

My donkey has a headache and the doctor
   has given him a thick cap/chunky knit cap,
   my donkey is ill.

My donkey has earache and the doctor has
   given him a jug of beer, my donkey is ill.

My donkey has a sore throat and the doctor
   has given him a white scarf, my donkey is ill.

My donkey has heartache and the doctor has
   given him lemon drops, my donkey is ill.

My donkey has knee ache/a pain in the knees
   and the doctor has given him a small flask/
   bottle of tablets/pills, my donkey is ill.

La Tarara page 96
La Tarara

La Tarara has a white dress that she only wears
   on Maundy Thursday.
La Tarara yes, La Tarara no, La Tarara, mother, I
   dance to it.

La Tarara has a pair of trousers that from top to
   bottom they are all buttons/they are
   covered in buttons.
La Tarara yes, La Tarara no, La Tarara, mother, I
   dance to it.

La Tarara has a green dress full of flounces/
   ruffles and little bells.
La Tarara yes, La Tarara no, La Tarara, mother, I
   dance to it.

This is a very old song. In Spanish we have a
saying 'as old as La Tarara' – 'tan viejo como La
Tarara'. It seems that La Tarara was a very
eccentric woman, who wore strange things. The
phrase 'La Tarara madre que la bailo yo' refers
to the song itself, to the dance in the song.

Vocabulario – Key words

a

abril(m)	April
aburrido(m)	boring
adiós(m)	goodbye
agosto(m)	August
agua(sin. m. pl. f)	water
agua mineral(as above)	mineral water
al(a+el)	to
alemán	German
Alemania	Germany
alfombra(f)	rug
allá	over there
allí	there
amarillo	yellow
animal(m)	animal
animales domésticos(m.pl)	pets
año(m)	year
aparcamiento(m)	parking
aquí	here
aquí tiene	here you are
araña(f)	spider
ático(m)	attic
autobús(m)	bus
avión(m)	plane
azul	blue

b

banco(m)	bank
bandera(f)	flag
barco(m)	boat
bastante difícil	quite difficult
bicicleta(f)	bicycle
blanco	white
boca(f)	mouth
bocadillo(m)	baguette
bolígrafo(m)	pen
brazo(m)	arm
buen viaje	have a good trip

c

caballo(m)	horse
cabeza(f)	head
café(m)	café/coffee
calcetines(m. pl)	socks
cama(f)	bed
camisa(f)	shirt
camiseta(f)	T-shirt
campo(m)	countryside
canción(f)	song
cantar	to sing
cartera(f)	school bag
casa(f)	house
catorce	fourteen
chaqueta(f)	jacket
chocolate(m)	chocolate
cinco	five
Coca-Cola(f)	coke

coche(m)	car
cocina(f)	kitchen
comedor(m)	dining room
comer	to eat
comisaría(f)	police station
como	I eat
¿cómo estás?	how are you?
¿cómo te llamas?	what is your name?
compañero(m)	mate/pal
completar	to complete
conejo(m)	rabbit
conejo de indias(m)	guinea pig
copiar	to copy
corbata(f)	tie
correos(m)	post office
corto	short
croissant(m)	croissant
cuaderno(m)	exercise book
cuando	when
¿cuántos años tienes?	how old are you?
cuarto de baño(m)	bathroom
cuatro	four
cumpleaños(m)	birthday

d

dar	to give
de	of, from
¿de qué color es ...?	what colour is ...?
derecha	right
día(m)	day
día de la madre	mother's day
día libre	day off
dibujar	to draw
dibujo(m)	drawing/picture
diciembre(m)	December
diecinueve	nineteen
dieciocho	eighteen
dieciséis	sixteen
diecisiete	seventeen
diez	ten
divertido	fun
doce	twelve
doce de octubre	12th October
domingo(m)	Sunday
¿dónde está ...?	where is ...?
¿dónde vas?	where are you going?
dormitorio(m)	bedroom
dos	two

e

el(m)	the
en	in, on
encontrar	to find
educación física(f)	physical education

¡Es Español!   © Kathy Williams and Beatriz Rubio

enero	January	Inglaterra	England
es	it is/she is/he is	inglés	English
escocés	Scottish	interesante	interesting
Escocia	Scotland	invierno(m)	winter
escribir	to write	Irlanda	Ireland
escuchar	to listen	Irlanda del Norte	Northern Ireland
escuela(f)	school	irlandés	Irish
España	Spain	Italia	Italy
Español	Spanish	italiano	Italian
ésta es ...(f)	this is ...	izquierda	left
estación(f)	station	**j**	
éste es ...(m)	this is ...	jamón(m)	ham
estómago(m)	stomach	jueves(m)	Thursday
estoy bien	I am fine	jugar	to play
estrella(f)	star	julio(m)	July
estuche(m)	pencil case	junio(m)	June
estupendo	super	**k**	
f		kilómetro	kilometre
falda(f)	skirt	**l**	
febrero(m)	February	la(f)	the
Feliz Año Nuevo	Happy New Year	lápiz	pencil
Feliz Navidad	Merry Christmas	largo	long
fiesta	party/celebration	las(f. pl)	the
francés	French	leer	to read
Francia	France	levantarse	to get up
g		lindo	cute
galés	Welsh	los(m. pl)	the
garaje(m)	garage	lunes(m)	Monday
gato(m)	cat	**ll**	
geografía	geography	llegar	to arrive
goma(f)	rubber	llevar	to wear
gracias	thank you	llueve	it rains
grande	big	**m**	
gris	grey	madre(f)	mother
gustar	to like	mano(f)	hand
h		mantequilla(f)	butter
hablar	to talk/speak	manzana(f)	apple
hace bueno	it is fine	marrón	brown
hace calor	it is hot	martes(m)	Tuesday
hace frío	it is cold	matemáticas(f.pl)	maths
hace malo	it is not a nice day	mayo(m)	may
hace sol	it is sunny	me gusta	I like
hace viento	it is windy	me llamo ...	my name is ...
hacer	to do	me quedo	I stay
hago	I do	mes(m)	month
hermana(f)	sister	mesa(f)	table
hermano(m)	brother	mi(singular)	my
historia(f)	history	mi cumpleaños es ...	my birthday is ...
hola	hello	mi dirección es ...	my address is ...
hombro(m)	shoulder	miércoles	Wednesday
hora(f)	time/hour	mi horario	my timetable
hotel(m)	hotel	mirar	to look (at)
hoy	today	mis(pl)	my
i		mi tiempo libre	my free time
iglesia(f)	church	montaña(f)	mountain
informática	ICT/computers	monumento(m)	monument

moreno	brown(hair, complexion)	quiero	I want/I would like?
muñeco de nieve(m)	snowman	quince	fifteen
museo(m)	museum	**r**	
música(f)	music	ratón(m)	mouse
n		regalo(m)	present
naranja	orange	regla (f)	ruler
nariz(f)	nose	rellenar	to fill
Navidad(f)	Christmas	reno(m)	reindeer
negro	black	repetir	to repeat
nieva	it snows	responder	respond/answer
Nochebuena(f)	Christmas Eve	rodilla(f)	knee
Nochevieja(f)	New Year's Eve	rojo	red
no	no	rosa	pink
no me gusta	I don't like	rubio	blond
no tengo	I don't have	**s**	
noviembre(m)	November	sábado(m)	Saturday
nueve	nine	sacapuntas(m)	pencil sharpener
número	number	salón(m)	lounge
o		sandwich(m)	sandwich
		seis	six
ocho	eight	semana(f)	week
octubre(m)	October	Semana Santa(f)	Easter
ojo(m)	eye	sentarse	to sit down
once	eleven	septiembre(m)	September
oreja(f)	ear	sí	yes
otoño(m)	autumn	siete	seven
p		silla(f)	chair
padre(m)	father	sombrero(m)	hat
país(m)	country	soy	I am
País de Gales	Wales	**t**	
pájaro(m)	bird	té	tea
pan(m)	bread	¿te gusta ...?	do you like ...?
pantalones(m.pl)	trousers	trabajar	to work
Papá Noel	Father Christmas	trece	thirteen
patatas fritas(f.pl)	crisps/chips	treinta	thirty
pelo(m)	hair	tren	train
pequeño	small	tres	three
perdone	excuse me	**v**	
perrito caliente(m)	hot dog	vaqueros(m. pl)	jeans
perro(m)	dog	veinte	twenty
pez(m)	fish	verano(m)	summer
pie(m)	foot	verde	green
pierna(f)	leg	vestíbulo(m)	hall
piscina(f)	swimming pool	vestido(m)	dress
playa(f)	beach	viernes(m)	Friday
primavera(f)	spring	vivo en ...	I live in ...
q		volver	to return
quedarse	to stay	voy	I go
¿qué es?	what is it?	**y**	
queso(m)	cheese	yo	I
¿qué tiempo hace?	what is the weather like?	**z**	
		Zapatillas de deporte(f. pl)	trainers
¿qué van a tomar?	what are you going to have?	zapatos(m. pl)	shoes
		zumo(m)	juice
¿quién es?	who is it?	zumo de fruta(m)	fruit juice

¡Es Español! © Kathy Williams and Beatriz Rubio